AF423360

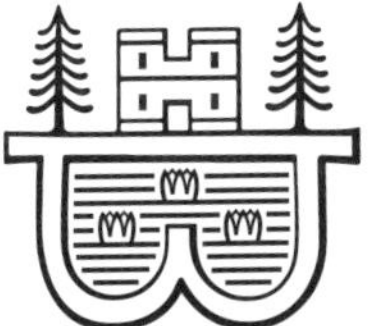

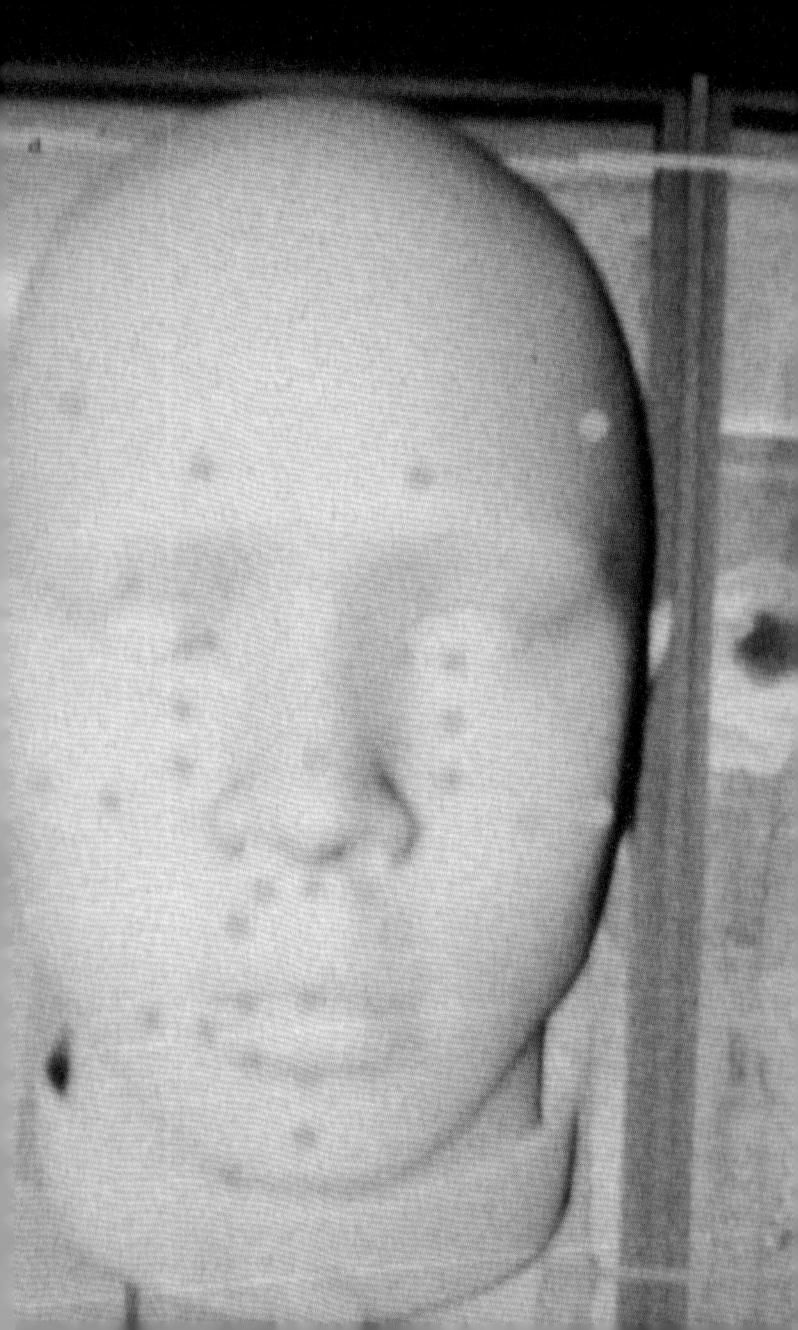

Edited by / Herausgegeben von
Anna Gritz

Jenna Bliss

Haus am Waldsee
Spector Books

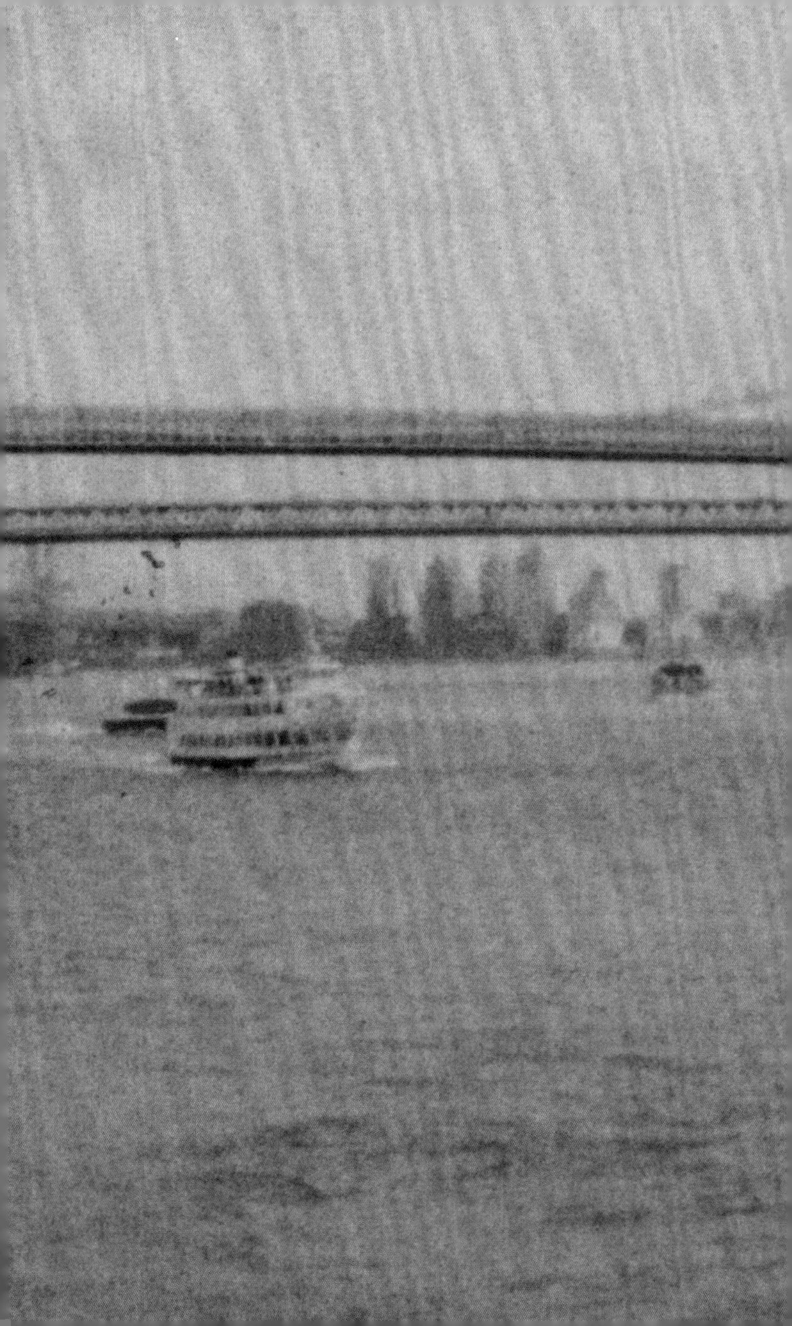

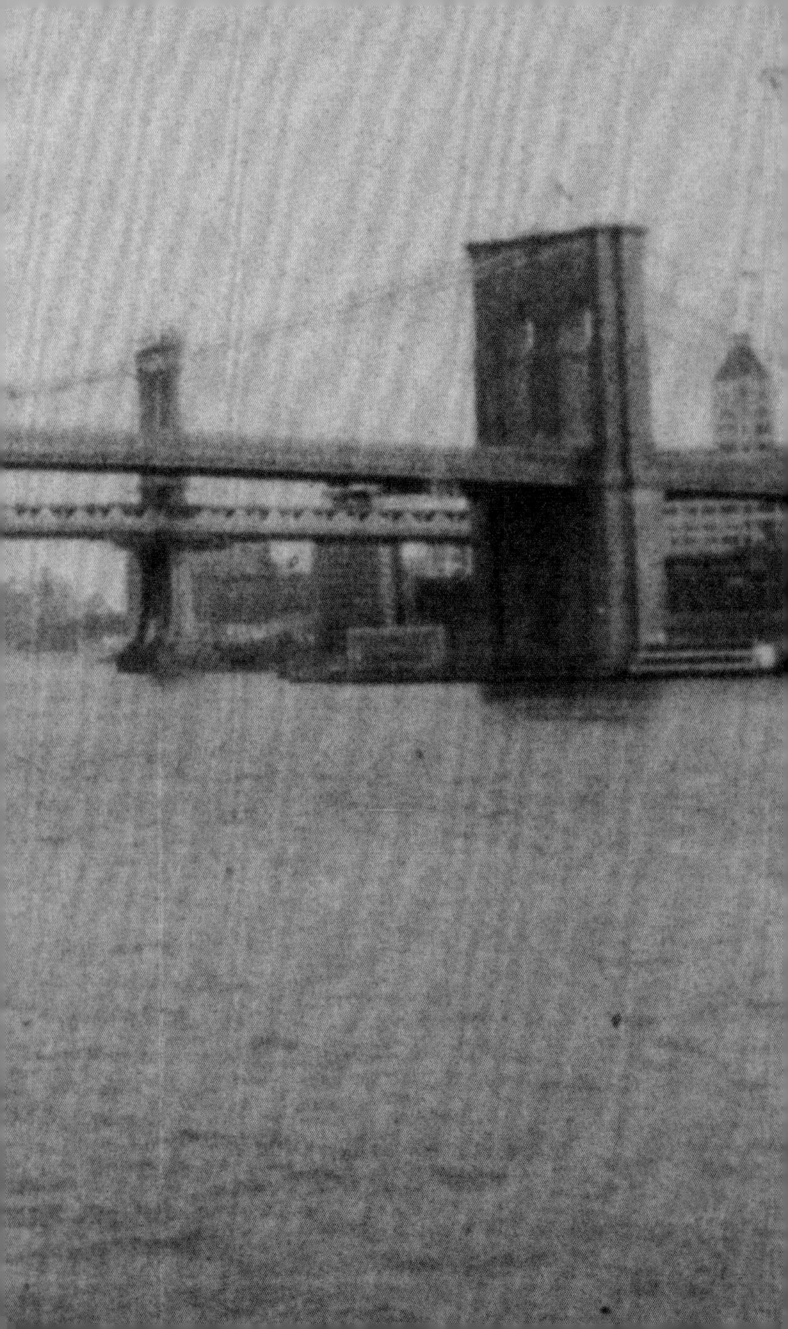

Foreword / Vorwort
Anna Gritz

*

Little brown band-aids were carefully stuck to our ear cartilage, each containing a small seed that applied soft pressure, stimulating points that, according to what is known as auriculotherapy, can relieve pain, stress, and other ailments. In a heightened state of physical and spatial awareness we entered the screening.

This little self-help exercise was the preamble to a fragmentary presentation of Jenna Bliss's *The People's Detox*, which I organized in my then role as curator at South London Gallery in 2014 (the work was released in its final form in 2018). The film explores the history of a revolutionary drug clinic in the South Bronx in New York City that was set up in the 1970s by the Puerto Rican political organization the Young Lords, revolutionary health collectives, and local addicts, and that profoundly transformed contemporary notions of health and addiction care through the inclusion of alternative treatments such as acupuncture. More than that, however, the film also revealed structural state involvement in the peddling of drugs in the Bronx and elsewhere, effectively fueling a pandemic of addiction. Bliss assembled a mix of interviews with eye witnesses and archival material in the form of an experimental documentary that she produced over the course of several years. At the time of the presentation, the film was still very much in development, to the point that the screening could be considered part of the process. The event was bookended by a communal tai chi workout guided by Bliss and lit by a large spotlight in the shape of a yin and yang symbol that shone down through a skylight and cast half of the participants in bright light and the other half in darkness.

Years later, in 2017, Jenna Bliss and I worked together again, then at KW Institute for Contemporary Art in Berlin, where I invited her to devise a series of events alongside the screening of her film *Poison the Cure* (2017). The work examines deliberate and enforced drug use in the US and its territories. Once again through collaging archival material, animation, and scripted scenes, Bliss draws an analogy between the recreational consumption of opiates and morphine in nineteenth-century New York City and the birth control trials enforced upon female factory workers in Puerto Rico in the mid-twentieth century. *Nihilism and Self Care*, as the series of events was titled, consisted in informal private and semi-private gatherings based on "the realities of life in destruction: of the planet, public spheres, the common good, and our own atomized bodies," as Bliss stated. As part of one of the events, mimicking feminist public-consciousness-raising sessions of the 1970s, I saw my own cervix for the first time; other formats brought together thinkers and artists working in Berlin around issues of gender, reproduction, and health autonomy. These expanded forms of screenings pre-empted a methodology that today has become representative of Bliss's work: her tendency to borrow, restage, and assimilate aesthetics, research, practices, and technologies stemming from the time periods of her research material, mining them for their unique characteristics, and then, through montage, eliciting the materials' inherent ideologies.

Bliss's choice of subject matter is often influenced by the locations that she explores during her regular long walks and perambulations. The moving image that she habitually records on Super 8 film during excursions is akin to keeping a sketchbook. This material is then met with meticulous research, which brings together historical details, intuitive associations, and personal and collective memories, thus expanding on official narratives while questioning common assumptions. Her focus is frequently drawn to historically loaded topics that are lodged in the built structure of New York City, ranging from addiction and the pharmaceutical industry to the aftermath of 9/11 and the global economic crisis of 2007/08. Again and again in her long-format films, photographs, short videos, and sculptures, the artist unites personal impressions, encounters, and observations from her daily life, and traces their far-reaching associations in order to re-evaluate narratives as well as formal and aesthetic dimensions that are taken for granted. Even when working with archival or found footage, Bliss's works have the aura of something staged in the guise of a period drama. This is not necessarily due to their emotional charge, but rather to Bliss's ability to digest a particular time, its codes and aesthetics, in a way that reveals repressed plots. She directs the material to perform itself, and, in doing so, reveals subliminal messaging and stand-ins for larger political developments that only the distance of time makes palpable and whose effects are still felt today.

Bliss's current work focuses on the recent history of Wall Street and the far-reaching consequences of high-risk financial speculation. She imagines that the various fragments will eventually form a series including at least one feature-length film: a history of Wall Street shutdown and the institution's propensity to be at the center of disasters that affected New York City, and whose consequences were felt world-wide—most notably, 9/11, the economic crisis of 2007/08, Hurricane Sandy, as well as the political protest movements formed in their wake. The exhibition at Haus am Waldsee assembles the first two bodies of work in this series, focusing on 9/11 on the one hand, and the financial crash of 2008 on the other. Both incidents are explored by means of constellations of work that investigate their subjects through a mixture of fact and fiction, abstraction and detail, painting a far-sighted portrait that allows larger patterns to emerge.

The power dynamics inherent in the format of the panorama, as employed in Bliss's sequence of sweeping views of the skyline of New York City in the two series *Panorama* and *Drone* (both 2021), evidence the privileged access to vistas that underlie claims of property and illustrate visions of monopoly, power, and control. *Panorama* recalls early photographic experiments by Eadweard Muybridge such as the 360-degree panoramic display of San Francisco from 1878. At the time, the city was in a period of ravenous growth, fueled by a gold rush that turned the men behind the Central Pacific Railroad—Mark Hopkins, Leland Stanford, Charles Crocker, and Collis Potter Huntington—into the ultra-rich of their era. All four built grandiose mansions on what is now known as Nob Hill, a neighborhood offering sprawling views of the city. It was this landscape of power that Muybridge captured in his photographs. Curiously, Muybridge's panorama is void of actual life, its grand scale and long exposure time effectively erasing anything in motion. The absence of life renders it desolate, conjuring a time after the boom. After completing the panorama, Muybridge became fully immersed in the motion studies that would forever cast him as a forefather of early cinema. Much later, he retired to Kingston upon Thames in his native England, resorting to gardening as his pastime. When he died in 1904, he was said to have been in the process of constructing a pond that mirrored the outlines of the Great Lakes of North America as seen from an aerial perspective. Two years later, in 1906, San Francisco suffered a devastating earthquake and fire that killed at least three thousand residents and destroyed an estimated eighty percent of the city, and with it the ostentatious mansions of the railroad barons.

Perspectives that allow for distance—such as the images from the *Panorama* and *Drone* series which were taken from the top of One World Trade and the Empire State Building—occupy much of Bliss's work. She shares this interest in critical distances with Carol Rhodes, the Glaswegian artist whose paintings and drawings are presented in the first-floor galleries of the Haus am Waldsee. Both artists have a habit of allowing fact and fiction to collide in their work in order to make the larger bearing of structural human intervention tangible. Seeing them in parallel opens up correspondences between their practices in addition to activating the institution in its own historical and spatial intertwining with ideological perspectives.

I have followed the progress of Jenna Bliss's artistic practice with much admiration and respect for over ten years now, and it is a great honor for me to present this significant overview of her latest bodies of work here at the Haus am Waldsee. My sincere thanks go above all to Jenna for her trust and hard work and for creating a body of work which makes me realize that each step into the world is supported by a million assumptions, all of which can be questioned, leaving us with a beautifully shaky ground to walk on. Particular thanks also go to my colleagues Beatrice Hilke, who curated Carol Rhodes' exhibition alongside this one, and who allowed Rhodes' practice to rub against Bliss's work in such a striking and rewarding manner, and Pia-Marie Remmers, curatorial assistant at the Haus am Waldsee, for her endless effort, her commitment, and the vital insights she brought to the production of both exhibitions. I am delighted that this publication features a major new essay by Ivan Gaytan, and I thank him for his passionate and profound insight into Jenna Bliss's practice. I am also deeply grateful to Benedikt Reichenbach's intelligent and empathetic design for this publication, developed in close conversation with Jenna and Ivan. I also wish to thank Eva Wilson for her invaluable editorial input. Further, I would like to thank the translators Michèle Graf and Selina Grüter, as well as the copyeditors Cordelia Marten, Anna Siebold, and Tina Wessel.

I am, moreover, indebted to the dedicated staff at the Haus am Waldsee. It is their hard work and expertise that made the realization of these exhibitions possible in the first place and it is their astuteness and enthusiasm that allow the spirit of the exhibitions to be carried through the entire institution. My sincere thanks go to Sarah Albrecht, Linus Cuno von Aufsess, Tobias Bader, Luise Bichler, Michael Gottberg, Erik Günther, Valentin Hesch, Samer Ismail, Sebastian Jefford, Carl-Oskar Jonsson, Mette Kleinsteuber, Martina Kutsch, Sarah Mohr, Jeannette Mügge, Johanna Pistorius, Claire Rüffer, Nele Schinz, Swenja Schmidt, Regina Schreieder, Anna Schulte, Wiebke Sünderhauf, Frederik Worm, and Yvonne Zindel. I would also like to thank the restorer Wolfram Gabler for his many years of expert support for the Haus am Waldsee. The exhibitions and the accompanying publications by Jenna Bliss and Carol Rhodes were made possible by a grant from the Capital Cultural Fund Berlin and the Association of Friends and Supporters—Haus am Waldsee e.V., to whom we are greatly indebted.

Sorgfältig wurden kleine, braune Pflaster mit je einem winzigen Samen darin auf unsere Ohrmuscheln geklebt, um dort sanften Druck auszuüben und Punkte zu stimulieren, die gemäß der sogenannten Aurikulotherapie Schmerz, Stress und andere Leiden lindern können. Auf diese Weise in einen höheren physischen und räumlichen Bewusstseinszustand versetzt, betraten wir die Filmvorführung.

Diese kleine Selbsthilfeübung stellte die Präambel zu einer fragmentarischen Präsentation von Jenna Bliss' *The People's Detox* dar, die ich 2014 in meiner damaligen Funktion als Kuratorin der South London Gallery organisiert hatte (in finaler Form wurde das Werk schließlich 2018 veröffentlicht). Der Film beleuchtet die Geschichte einer wegweisenden Klinik für Drogenabhängige, die in den 1970er Jahren im New Yorker Stadtteil South Bronx von der puerto-ricanischen politischen Organisation Young Lords gemeinsam mit Kollektiven für revolutionäre Gesundheitsfürsorge und lokalen Drogenabhängigen gegründet wurde. Durch die Einführung alternativer Behandlungen wie Akupunktur hat sie das damalige Verständnis von medizinischer Versorgung und Suchthilfe grundlegend verändert. Der Film enthüllt darüber hinaus, inwiefern der Staat damals an der Verbreitung von Drogen in der Bronx und andernorts beteiligt war und regelrecht eine Abhängigkeitspandemie anheizte. Bliss montierte verschiedene Interviews mit Augenzeug*innen und Archivmaterial zu einem experimentellen Dokumentarfilm, den sie über mehrere Jahre hinweg produzierte. Zum Zeitpunkt der Veranstaltung war der Film noch in der Entwicklungsphase und seine Vorführung gewissermaßen Teil dieses Prozesses. Den Abschluss des Abends bildete ein gemeinsames Tai-Chi-Training unter Bliss' Anleitung. Ein großer Scheinwerfer strahlte das Yin-und-Yang-Symbol ab und tauchte eine Hälfte der Teilnehmenden in helles, die andere Hälfte in dunkles Licht.

2017 arbeiteten Jenna Bliss und ich erneut zusammen. Dieses Mal hatte ich sie dazu eingeladen, für die KW Institute for Contemporary Art in Berlin eine begleitende Veranstaltungsreihe zu ihrem Film *Poison the Cure* (2017) zu entwickeln. Das Werk untersucht sowohl den vorsätzlichen als auch den erzwungenen Drogenkonsum in den USA und ihren Außengebieten. Auch hier zieht Bliss mittels Collagen aus Archivmaterial, Animationen und gescripteten Szenen Analogien zwischen dem Freizeitkonsum von Opiaten und Morphium im New York des 19. Jahrhunderts und den Verhütungsmittelexperimenten, die in den 1950er Jahren in Puerto Rico an Fabrikarbeiterinnen durchgeführt wurden. *Nihilism and Self Care*, so der Titel der Veranstaltungsreihe, bestand aus privaten und halb öffentlichen Treffen, die sich, wie Bliss erklärte, um die „Realität eines in Zerstörung befindlichen Lebens" drehten, um „die Zerstörung des Planeten, des öffentlichen Lebens, der gemeinschaftlichen Güter und unserer eigenen atomisierten Körper". Bei einer der Veranstaltungen, die an feministische Sessions zur Stärkung eines öffentlichen Bewusstseins der 1970er Jahre anknüpfte, sah ich meinen eigenen Gebärmutterhals zum ersten Mal; andere Formate brachten Berliner Denker*innen und Künstler*innen zusammen, die sich mit Fragen von Gender, Reproduktion und gesundheitlicher Unabhängigkeit befassen. Diese über einfache Screenings hinausgehenden Veranstaltungen nahmen damals bereits eine Methodologie vorweg, die für Bliss' Werk heute typisch ist: ihre Tendenz, die Ästhetik, Forschung, Praxis und Technologie dem Zeitraum ihres Forschungsmaterials zu entlehnen, alles aufzunehmen und neu zu inszenieren, charakteristische Eigenschaften zu durchleuchten und schließlich die dem Material inhärenten Ideologien durch Montage herauszufiltern.

Nicht selten beeinflussen die Orte, die Bliss auf ihren regelmäßigen langen Spaziergängen und Streifzügen entdeckt, ihre Themenwahl. So gleichen die Bilder, die sie während ihrer Exkursionen auf Super-8-Film aufnimmt, einem Skizzenbuch. Das Material wird akribisch recherchiert, wobei historische Details, intuitive Assoziationen sowie persönliche und kollektive Erinnerungen zusammenkommen; das offizielle Narrativ wird erweitert, während Bliss verbreitete Auffassungen hinterfragt. Ihr Fokus richtet sich dabei häufig auf historisch aufgeladene Themen, die tief in den Strukturen New Yorks verankert sind – diese reichen von Drogenabhängigkeit und der Pharmaindustrie bis zu den Folgen des 11. Septembers 2001 und der Weltfinanzkrise 2007/08. Immer wieder vereint die Künstlerin in ihren längeren Filmen, Fotografien, kürzeren Videos und Skulpturen ihre persönlichen Eindrücke, Begegnungen und Beobachtungen aus ihrem Alltag und spürt tiefgreifenden Zusammenhängen nach, um Narrative sowie formale und ästhetische Dimensionen, die für selbstverständlich gelten, neu zu bewerten. Selbst wenn Bliss mit vorgefundenem oder Archivmaterial arbeitet, wirken ihre Werke in Gestalt historischer Dramen doch inszeniert. Dies liegt nicht zwingend am emotionalen Charakter, sondern vielmehr an Bliss' Fähigkeit, bestimmte Zeiträume mit ihren Codes und ihrer Ästhetik so aufzuarbeiten, dass sich verdrängte Erzählungen offenbaren. Sie bringt das Material dazu, sich selbst zu entlarven, und enthüllt unterschwellige Bezüge und Hinweise größerer politischer Entwicklungen, die erst durch ihre zeitliche Distanz greifbar werden und bis heute ihre Wirkung zeigen.

In ihrem aktuellen Werk befasst sich Bliss mit der jüngeren Historie der Wall Street und den weitreichenden Folgen hochriskanter Finanzspekulation. Sie stellt sich vor, dass die verschiedenen Fragmente irgendwann eine Serie bilden und mindestens einen Spielfilm umfassen werden: eine Geschichte des Shutdowns der Wall Street und ihrer Tendenz, im Mittelpunkt jener Katastrophen in New York zu stehen, deren Folgen weltweit zu spüren waren – insbesondere des 11. Septembers, der Weltfinanzkrise 2007/08, des Hurrikans Sandy sowie der politischen Protestbewegungen, die sich daraufhin formierten. Die Ausstellung im Haus am Waldsee versammelt die ersten beiden Werkgruppen dieser Reihe, die sich mit dem 11. September und dem Finanzcrash von 2008 befassen. Beide Ereignisse werden in

Konstellationen von Werken untersucht, die ihre Motive durch eine Mischung aus Fakt und Fiktion, Abstraktion und Detail beleuchten und ein weitsichtiges Porträt zeichnen, das größere Muster erkennen lässt.

In den beiden Serien eindrücklicher Ansichten der New Yorker Skyline, *Panorama* und *Drone* (beide 2021), macht Bliss sich die Machtdynamik zunutze, die dem Panoramaformat anhaftet, belegt den privilegierten Zugang zu Ausblicken, dem Eigentumsansprüche zugrunde liegen, und illustriert Visionen von Monopol, Macht und Kontrolle. *Panorama* erinnert an die frühen fotografischen Experimente von Eadweard Muybridge, wie etwa die 360-Grad-Panoramaansicht von San Francisco aus dem Jahr 1878. Angeheizt durch den Goldrausch erlebte San Francisco zu dieser Zeit eine Phase rasanten Wachstums, die die Männer hinter der Central Pacific Railroad – Mark Hopkins, Leland Stanford, Charles Crocker und Collis Potter Huntington – zu den Superreichen jener Ära machten. Sie alle bauten imposante Villen im heutigen Nob Hill, dem Stadtteil mit einem atemberaubenden Blick auf die Stadt. Diese Landschaft der Mächtigen hielt Muybridge in seinen Fotografien fest. Seltsamerweise ist das echte Leben in Muybridges Panorama jedoch absent, denn durch den immensen Maßstab sowie die lange Belichtungszeit wurde jegliche Bewegung ausgelöscht. Die Abwesenheit von Leben lässt die Landschaft desolat erscheinen und erinnert an die Zeit nach dem Boom. Nach Vollendung des Panoramas widmete sich Muybridge voll und ganz seinen Bewegungsstudien, mit denen er sich auf ewig als Vorläufer des frühen Kinos in die Geschichte einschrieb. Jahre später zog er sich in seine englische Heimat Kingston upon Thames zurück, um sich der Gartenarbeit zu widmen. Als er 1904 starb, war er angeblich gerade dabei, einen Teich zu errichten, der die Umrisse der Großen Seen Nordamerikas aus der Luftperspektive widerspiegeln sollte. Nur zwei Jahre später, 1906, wurde San Francisco von einem verheerenden Erdbeben heimgesucht, das zusammen mit den dadurch verursachten Feuern mindestens 3.000 Anwohner*innen das Leben kostete und schätzungsweise achtzig Prozent der Stadt zerstörte, darunter auch die prunkvollen Villen der Eisenbahnbarone.

Perspektiven, die eine gewisse Distanz zulassen – wie die Bilder aus den Serien *Panorama* und *Drone*, die von der Spitze des One World Trade Center und des Empire State Building aufgenommen wurden –, nehmen in Bliss' Werk einen zentralen Platz ein. Dieses Interesse an kritischer Distanz teilt sie mit der Glasgower Künstlerin Carol Rhodes, deren Malereien und Zeichnungen im ersten Geschoss des Hauses am Waldsee zu sehen sind. Beide Künstlerinnen lassen Fakt und Fiktion in ihrem Werk aufeinanderprallen und verdeutlichen so die größere Tragweite struktureller menschlicher Eingriffe. Diese Gegenüberstellung eröffnet nicht nur eine Korrespondenz zwischen beiden Praktiken, sondern aktiviert das Haus am Waldsee auch in seiner eigenen historischen und räumlichen Verflechtung mit ideologischen Perspektiven.

Seit über zehn Jahren verfolge ich Jenna Bliss' künstlerische Praxis mit viel Bewunderung und Respekt. So ist es für mich eine große Ehre, diesen bedeutenden Überblick ihrer jüngsten Werkgruppen hier im Haus am Waldsee zu präsentieren. Mein aufrichtiger Dank gilt dabei in erster Linie Jenna für ihr Vertrauen und ihre unermüdliche Arbeit an einem Werk, das mir vor Augen führt, dass jeder Schritt in diese Welt von einer Million Annahmen getragen wird, die alle infrage gestellt werden können und uns auf einen wunderbar unsteten Boden zurückwerfen. Mein besonderer Dank gilt auch meinen Kolleginnen: Beatrice Hilke hat parallel die Ausstellung von Carol Rhodes kuratiert und ermöglicht, dass sich Rhodes' Praxis auf so eindrucksvolle und bereichernde Weise an Bliss' Werk reiben konnte. Die kuratorische Assistentin Pia-Marie Remmers hat sich mit unerschöpflichem Engagement und ihren unverzichtbaren Erkenntnissen in die Produktion beider Ausstellungen eingebracht. Außerdem bedanke ich mich bei Ivan Gaytan für seinen Essay in dieser Publikation, der uns einen sensiblen und tiefgründigen Einblick in die Praxis von Jenna Bliss ermöglicht. Mein Dank gilt auch Benedikt Reichenbach für die intelligente und einfühlsame

Gestaltung dieser Publikation, die in enger Zusammenarbeit mit Jenna und Ivan entstanden ist. Ich möchte auch Eva Wilson für ihren unschätzbaren editorischen Beitrag danken, ferner auch den Übersetzerinnen Michèle Graf und Selina Grüter und den Lektorinnen Cordelia Marten, Anna Siebold und Tina Wessel.

Darüber hinaus bin ich allen engagierten Mitarbeiter*innen des Hauses am Waldsee zu Dank verpflichtet. Ihre harte Arbeit sowie Expertise haben es ermöglicht, diese Ausstellungen zu realisieren; es ist ihrem Scharfsinn und Enthusiasmus zu verdanken, dass der Geist der Ausstellungen durch die gesamte Einrichtung hindurch spürbar ist. Mein herzlicher Dank geht an Sarah Albrecht, Linus Cuno von Aufsess, Tobias Bader, Luise Bichler, Michael Gottberg, Erik Günther, Valentin Hesch, Samer Ismail, Sebastian Jefford, Carl-Oskar Jonsson, Mette Kleinsteuber, Martina Kutsch, Sarah Mohr, Jeannette Mügge, Johanna Pistorius, Claire Rüffer, Nele Schinz, Swenja Schmidt, Regina Schreieder, Anna Schulte, Wiebke Sünderhauf, Frederik Worm und Yvonne Zindel. Danken möchte ich auch dem Restaurator Wolfram Gabler für seine langjährige fachliche Betreuung der Exponate des Hauses am Waldsee.

Die Ausstellungen und die begleitenden Publikationen von Jenna Bliss und Carol Rhodes wurden durch eine Förderung des Hauptstadtkulturfonds Berlin und des Vereins der Freunde und Förderer – Haus am Waldsee e.V. ermöglicht, denen wir hier unseren tiefsten Dank aussprechen möchten.

Correspondence
Ivan Gaytan

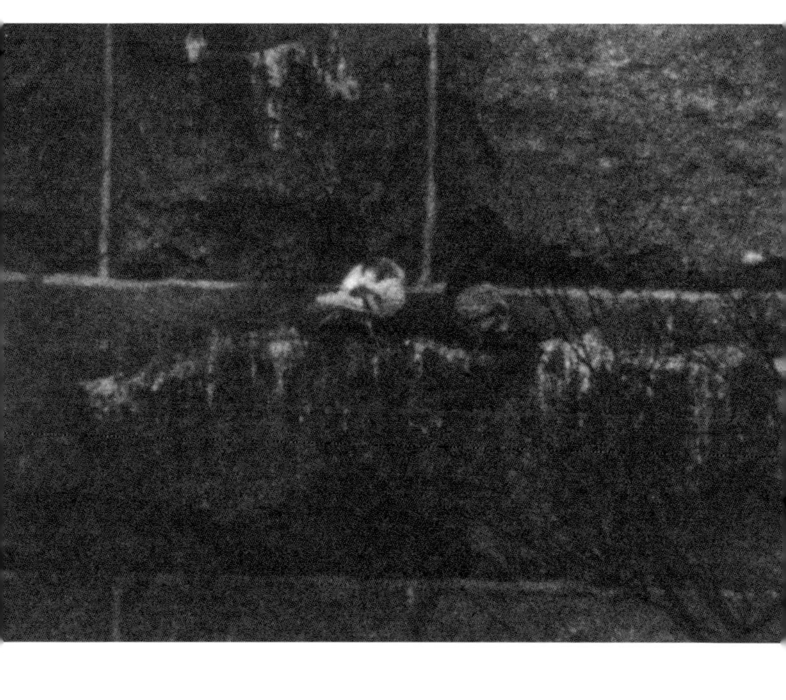

"In times of terror, when everyone is something of a conspirator, everybody will be in the position of having to play detective. Flânerie gives the individual the best prospects of doing so."

Walter Benjamin, "The Paris of the Second Empire in Baudelaire," in: id., *Selected Writings Volume 4: 1938–1940*, eds. Howard Eiland and Michael W. Jennings, trans. Harry Zohn (Cambridge, MA: Harvard University Press, 2003), p. 21.

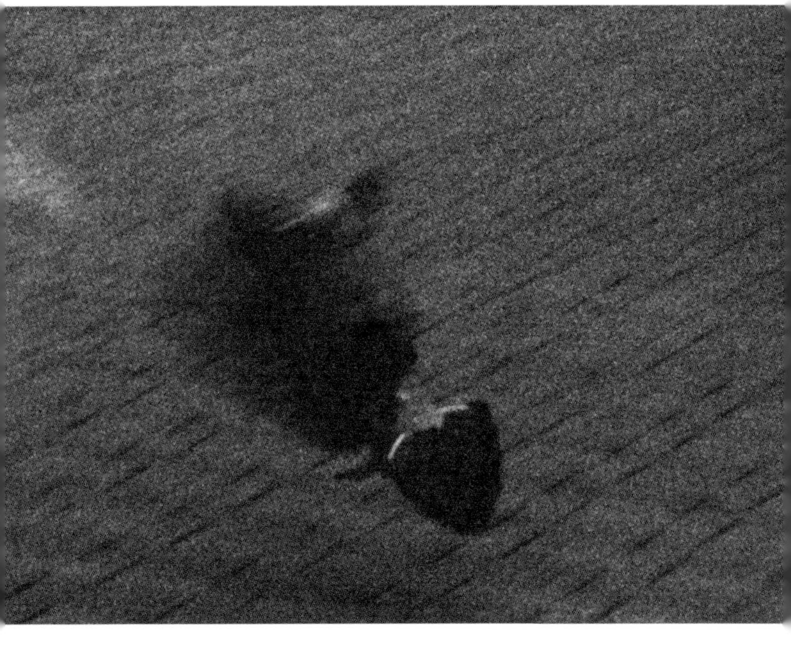

From my window I can see 200 West Street, 388 Greenwich, 60 Hudson Street, 33 Thomas Street, and 32 Avenue of the Americas, the latter a telecommunications building where Western Union, AT&T, and the New York Telephone Company were once found and where in the lobby there is now a Starbucks. One World Trade Center amid fog most evenings and the hotel at 27 Barclay are to the left, both casting at regular intervals shadows that fall across my desk. New York City is often perceived through a media-given sequence of its images, a fantasy of the city appearing much like the above-mentioned addresses, indicating a particular moment in the history of development in Lower Manhattan, or sooner found in its popular recognition through such phenomena as *Sex and the City*, the London plane tree (of the thousand species planted following Robert Moses's plans for the 1939/40 Flushing Meadows–Corona Park fair site), green benches and yellow taxis, Woody Allen, or *The Real Housewives*. How these images are collected and deployed to create a portrait of the city is the work of montage.

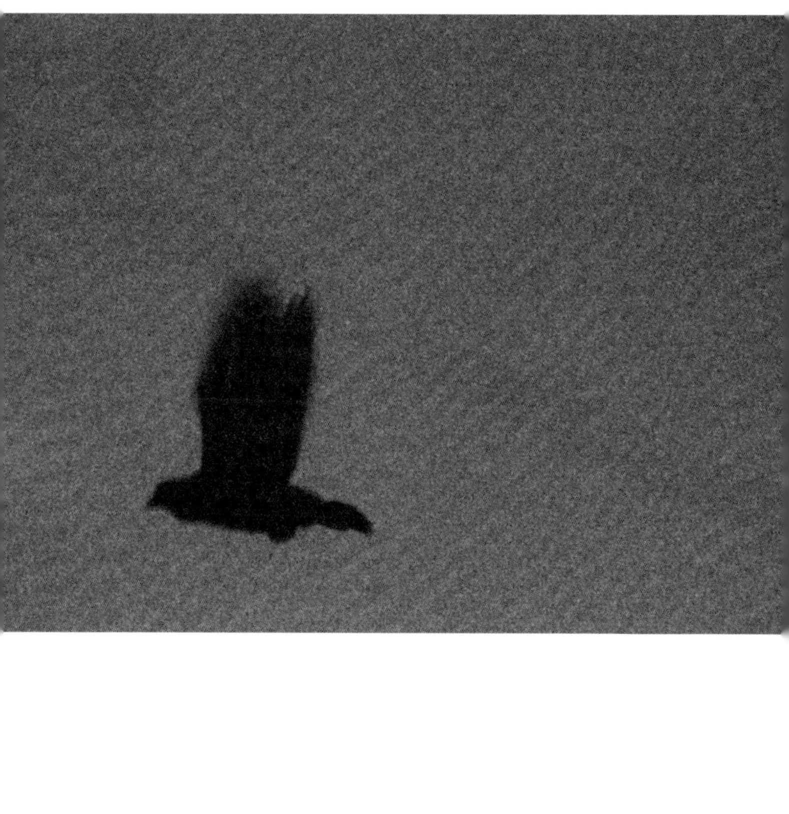

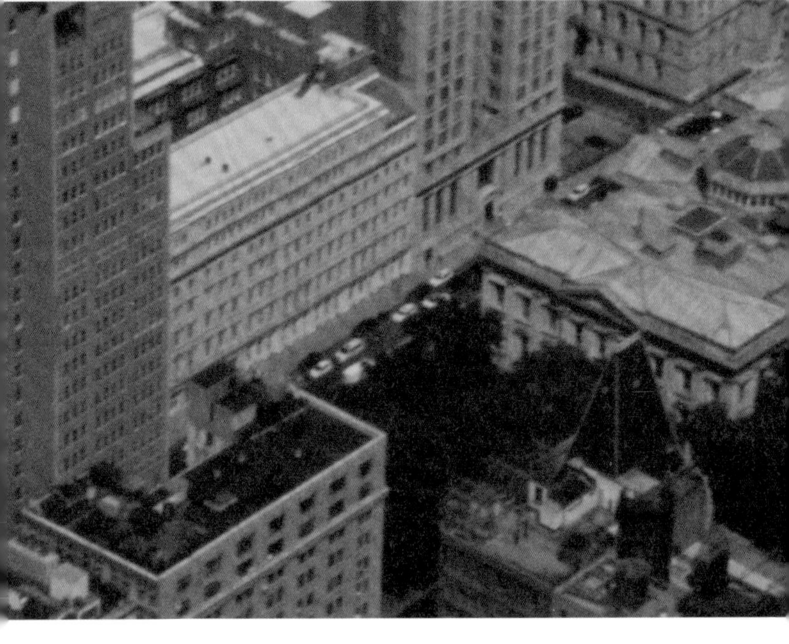

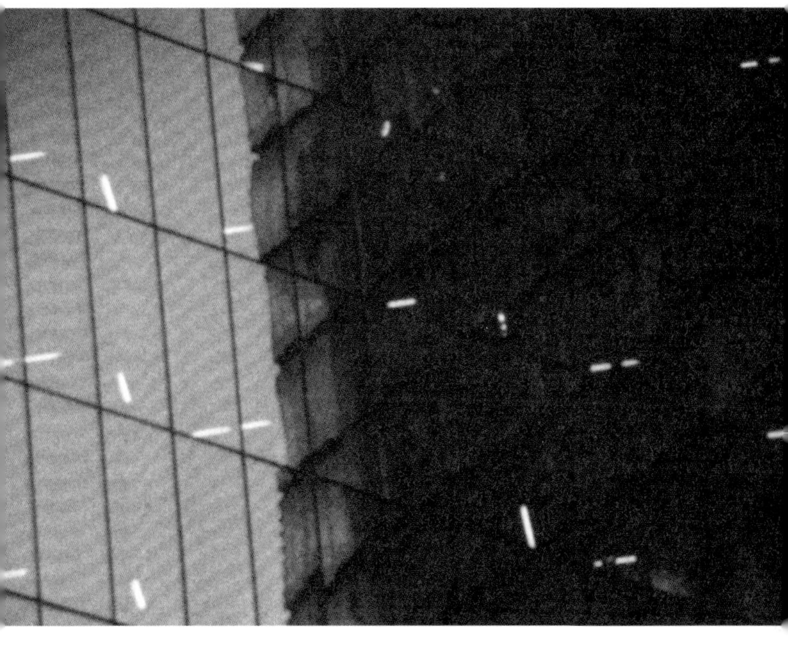

For instance, an image of the city can be found in a series of letters from 1937 to 1940: in a message from Denmark dated October 4, 1938, Detlef Holz writes to the Adornos that mounted in Brecht's son's room there is a plan for the city of Manhattan where on occasion he closely looks and imagines walking up and down the street of their apartment's address running parallel to the Hudson River. Along with such an idea of New York City, he may also imagine the slow movement of the ice floes visible that winter from the thirteenth-floor window of Gretel and Theodor Adorno's residency in exile, full of furniture from Frankfurt and Berlin, including a riverfront facing desk, glass cupboard, typewriting table and chair, as well a collection of Detlef's published and unpublished essays having already arrived stateside. Addressing Walter Benjamin by his pen name, as she had done since their first messages in 1933, Gretel Adorno writes to Detlef in 1939 that she will be waiting for him at Pier 88, anticipating his arrival on the SS Champlain, and that they will set about visiting the sites of the barbarous foreign land and the World's Fair

together. Benjamin traces routes on the
plan for the city and marks addresses
in colored pencil: 45 Christopher Street,
290 Riverside Drive, 429 W 117th Street,
he writes "Newyork" for New York City.

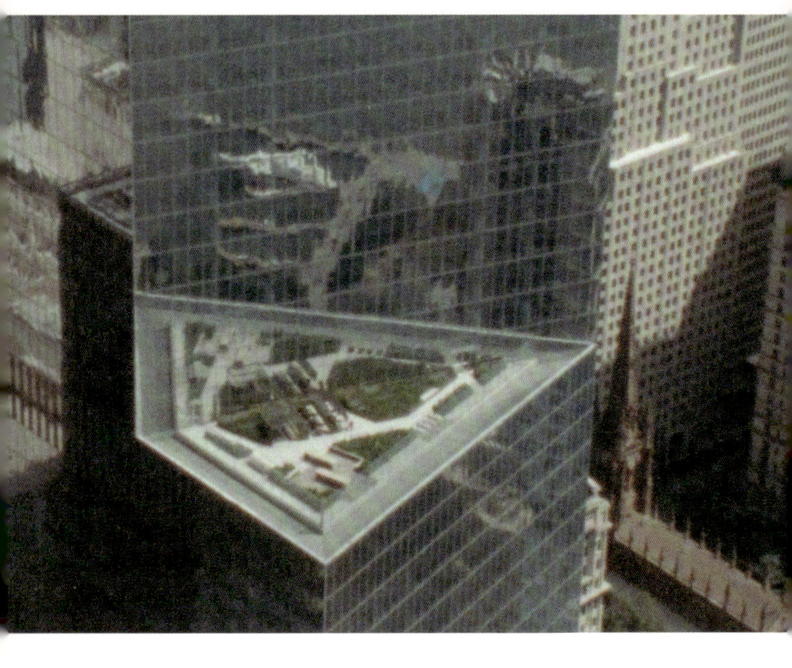

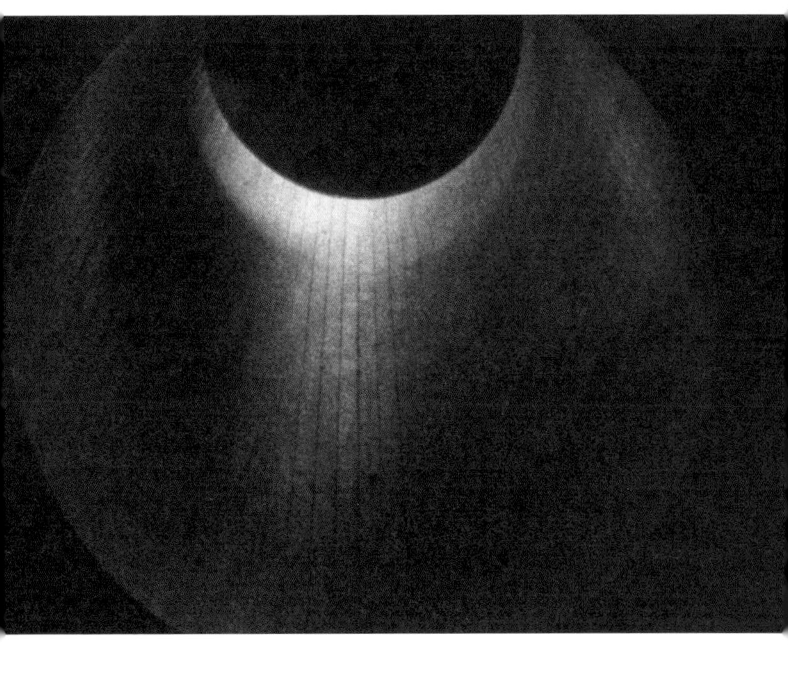

This correspondence concerning Benjamin's possible emigration to the city and its eventual faltering coincides with his collecting of a series of notes under the title *Central Park*, the ongoing assemblage of materials for *The Arcades Project*, and the numerous rewrites of the piece that would eventually be published as "On Some Motifs in Baudelaire" in the *Zeitschrift für Sozialforschung* in 1939. The concepts found in these late works would likely have received further expression in a lecture on aesthetic theory to be given at the invitation of Meyer Schapiro at Columbia University in 1940, and though Benjamin never gave this lecture, I often wonder what would have become of them if he walked the city in the 1940s as he intended to. How would the images of New York found in their letters have compared to an experience of the apparent lack of ice floes, the blocks of imposing high-rises, the fog which on occasion enshrouds the tops of buildings in their entirety, the pigeon congress that occurs under awnings and on streetcorners, the horizontal moon, or the absence of any stars at all?

By the summer of 1940 it was clear that
the decision to emigrate to New York, for
Benjamin, was untenable. Unwilling to de-
part from the Bibliothèque Nationale and the
Angelus Novus in his living room at 10 Rue
Dombasle, choosing neither Jerusalem nor
New York City, the continuing work on
his *Arcades* made Paris the only option
despite its worsening political conditions.
The main reading room and the print collection at the New York Public Library
would not have been in competition with
a room containing Victor Hugo manuscripts
at arm's reach, but it may have sufficed
for a time. He would have likely visited the
large dioramas depicting the skyline of the
city at the 1939/40 New York World's Fair
in Queens or gone multiple times to see
the billboards in Times Square with Gretel
Adorno at his side.

"World fairs glorify the exchange value
of the commodity. They create a framework
in which its use value becomes secondary.
They are a school in which the masses,
forcibly excluded from consumption, are
imbued with the exchange value of com-
modities to the point of identifying with it:

'Do not touch the items on display.' World fairs thus provide access to a phantasmagoria which a person enters in order to be distracted. Within these *divertissements*, to which the individual abandons himself in the framework of the entertainment industry, he remains always an element of a compact mass […] led to that state of subjection which propaganda, industrial as well as political, relies on."

Walter Benjamin, "Paris, Capital of the Nineteenth Century: Exposé of 1939," in: id., *The Arcades Project*, prepared on the basis of the German volume, ed. Rolf Tiedemann, trans. Howard Eiland and Kevin McLaughlin, adapted by the author (Cambridge, MA, and London: Belknap Press, 1999), p. 18.

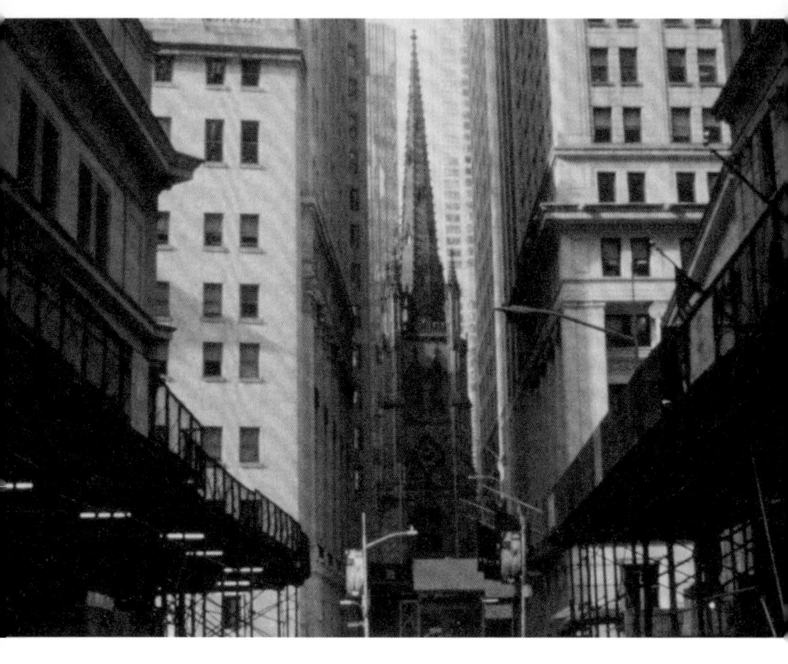

The city of Paris was conceived by
Benjamin through the presentation of what
was found in its arcades, where objects
appeared as if on a stage, allegorically ringing
out amid a crowd gathered in glassed-
in walkways; a writing dictated by a montage
principle that found its most acute realization in the first iteration of the Baudelaire
essay. And although I am not aware of any
particular affinity, many of the concepts
from this late period of Benjamin's writings
can be found in Jenna Bliss's depiction of
the city and its recent histories: the conspirator, in the approach to information and
its exchange; phantasmagoria, in the response
to various types of media and her utiliza-
tion of their forms; and allegory, in the use
of the fragment. In her work a portrait of
the city of New York is drawn tending specif-
ically toward melancholy, one instructed
by that very same montage principle that
Benjamin undertook in his explication of
iron and glass passages.

Bliss writes with the images that she records on regular walks in the city. The strategy of montage, deployed across the entirety of her oeuvre, stages the fragment as part of a larger narrative, each image becoming a propaedeutic to a work in progress—presented as if evidence of a larger plot. In *Drone II* and *Drone III* (both 2021), the World Trade Center station is seen bisected; it later reappears in 8mm as a backdrop to a bird in flight that is then transposed over a jet engine before landing on a table found in a nearby public plaza. It is all there: an image of a place and its histories is as legible as the reappearing flight path of the pigeon; connections fall into place from frame to frame and photograph to photograph. The fragments of image and language in Bliss's work chart a map of Manhattan where a building can appear as a symbol, sign, and finally, allegory. Facts appear before the camera lens as quickly as they are negated. Surfaces are captured that are capable of sustaining an idea of what occurs within them, what plots are being staged from their interior, just as easily as they represent the obfuscation

and complete blackout of information.
In *Spectacle* (2021), superimposition is employed to suggest the allegorical readability of the skyline or vacant office buildings kept perfunctorily lit, showing sites discussed in *Professional witnesses.* (2021) and functioning as a coda, we see images of the banal developments of commerce surrounding the Calatrava structure of the World Trade Center Transportation Hub, the NYSE, the moon, the Hudson at sunset, and a horizon of skyrises filmed from a waterfront construction site funded by a former New York governor who resigned in controversy. Leaves rustle from the fenced-in area and a pigeon takes off in flight soon after. In Bliss's assemblage of corporate logos, shop fronts, scaffolding, streetcorners, and workers, an image of the city seen as the seat of empire in the twenty-first century can be read, where plots, schemes, development, and political figures are cast together through the devising of the conspirator. In the first section of "The Paris of the Second Empire in Baudelaire," titled "I. Bohème," Benjamin writes that the nineteenth-century

conspirator had the barricade at the center of their movement: it established a commune, a camaraderie. So it is in the twenty-first century that the conspirator has placed information itself at the center of her work and is able to denote the recent past of New York City through a few key utterances: 9/11, CIA, Starbucks, airline stocks, Krongard. The references sit heavily within the presented constellation, and on video a directive: *Connecting the Dots*.

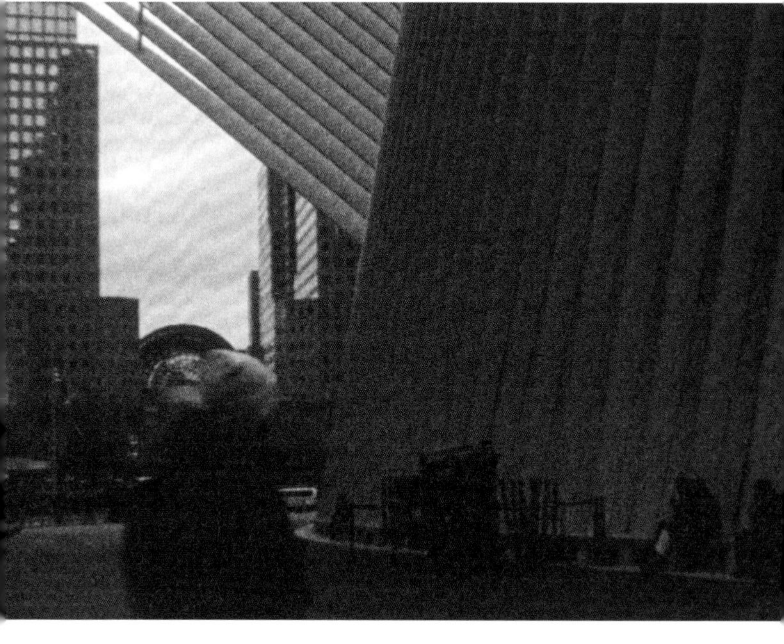

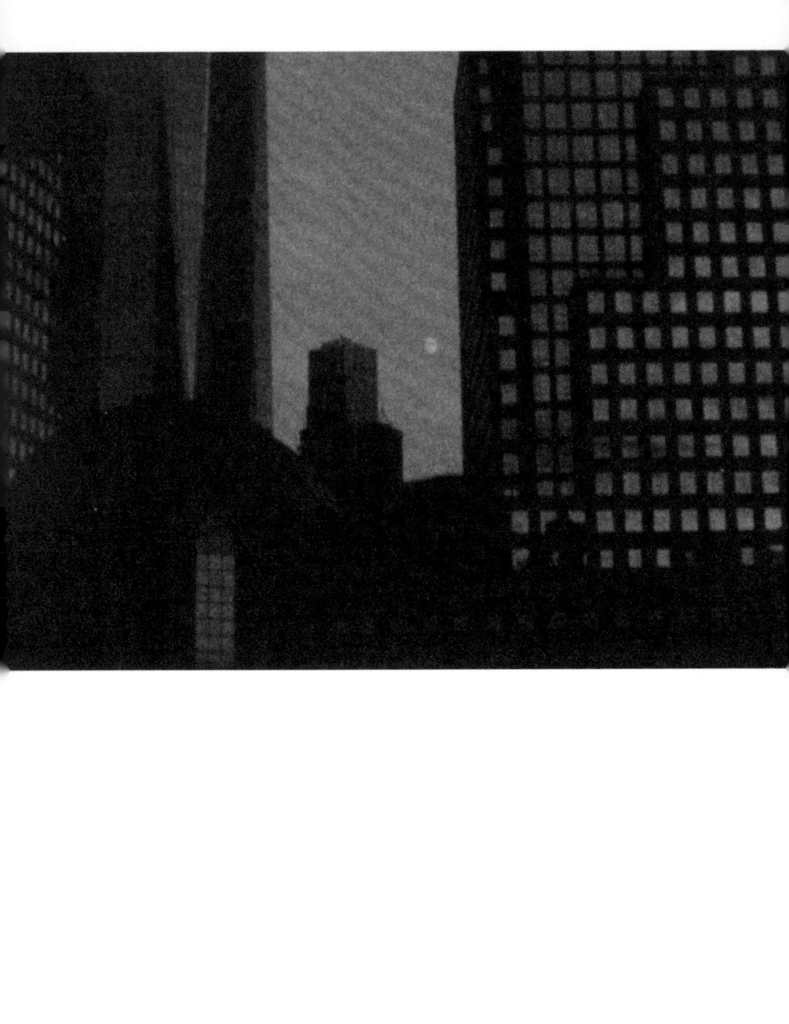

Bliss's works aim toward a correspondence to the lived reality of their capture, tempered by an understanding of the artifice of photography and the domination of spectacle over visuality—thus the decision to replicate the form of reality television and advertising. Her work counteracts the distracted nature in which ads and TV are typically received and their unassuming reception is instead confronted with a conspirator's discourse that can be read across Bliss's oeuvre. Instead of selling a product, they speak a subtle language of financial transactions, weapons deals, and Wall Street—such as in the testimonial *Professional witnesses.*, "todo está junto, con el gobierno, mucho noticiero, muchos periodistas …," or as the back-and-forth between collector and dealer at an art fair in *True Entertainment* (2023), "… full laundry service." They are not *Loose Change*, conspiracy films, but instead present images of the city in the plain language of actors on Bravo or MTV—or advertisements on either network. This is the antagonistic nature of Bliss's works: their basis in the commodity image, their destabilization through the indexical referencing of historical events found in their dialogue, and the argument, just as in the later writings of Benjamin, that these images are not to be interpreted as relics of dead history, propaganda, or mere fact, but instead must be considered through a "now of recognizability" where, as Benjamin writes, "the historical index of the images not only says that they belong to a particular time; it says, above all, that they attain to legibility only at a particular time. […] It is not that what is past casts its light on what is present, or what is present its light on what is past; rather, image is that wherein what has been comes together in a flash with the now to form a constellation. In other words: image is dialectics at a standstill. […] Only dialectical images are genuinely historical—that is, not archaic—images. The image that is read—which is to say, the image in the now of its recognizability—bears to the highest degree the imprint of the perilous critical moment on which all reading is founded."

Walter Benjamin, "N [On the Theory of Knowledge, Theory of Progress]," in: id., *The Arcades Project*, pp. 462–3.

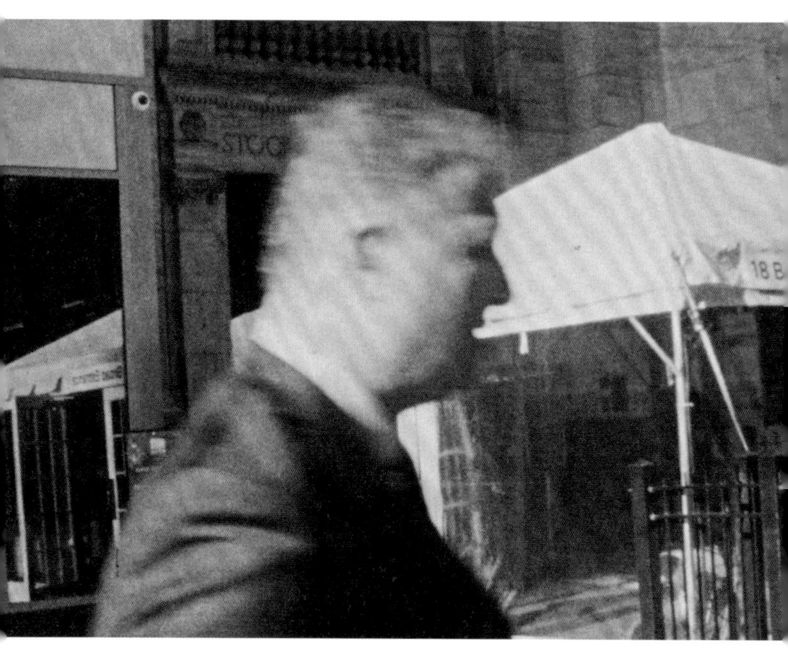
STOG
18 B

It is in the reverie of the flaneur, in Bliss's archive of political reality, social life, and wage labor, that an idea of the city is given as simply as the billboards in Times Square. In revisiting a familiar path, it would not be uncommon to follow in its entirety the demolition, stasis, and construction of a building, gaining an understanding of the structure by learning of the developers who proposed it, the financiers who fund it, the politicians who sanction it, and finally, the activities that take place within it: financial trading, a new jail, a luxury high-rise, or a shopping mall. The plazas that surround these sites are often made possible through laws that establish air rights incentives for real estate developers. These codes ultimately also afford protestors the ability to organize and occupy the parks and plazas where the developers' taste is often on view in the background nearby—Isa Genzken's *Rose III* and Mark di Suvero's *Joie de Vivre* in Zucotti Park, or Isamu Noguchi's *Red Cube* across the street. The city offers itself to a reading of its surfaces at every turn, and in recording the past five years, Bliss's films capture the abstract conditions of lived experience seen in protest-proofed doorways, co-working facilities, glass-faced reflective mirrors, and plazas gifted by the donor class. Suggested by these silent images is that an exact imagination of the city can be gained just as one might enter and exit a roundabout, integrating into the flow of the passers-by, mindful of the silent concordance that sustains traffic on the sidewalk and street.

"More and more relentlessly, the objective environment of human beings is coming to wear the expression of the commodity. At the same time, advertising seeks to disguise the commodity character of things. What resists the mendacious transfiguration of the commodity world is its distortion into allegory."

Walter Benjamin, "Central Park," in: id., *Selected Writings Volume 4: 1938–1940*, p. 173.

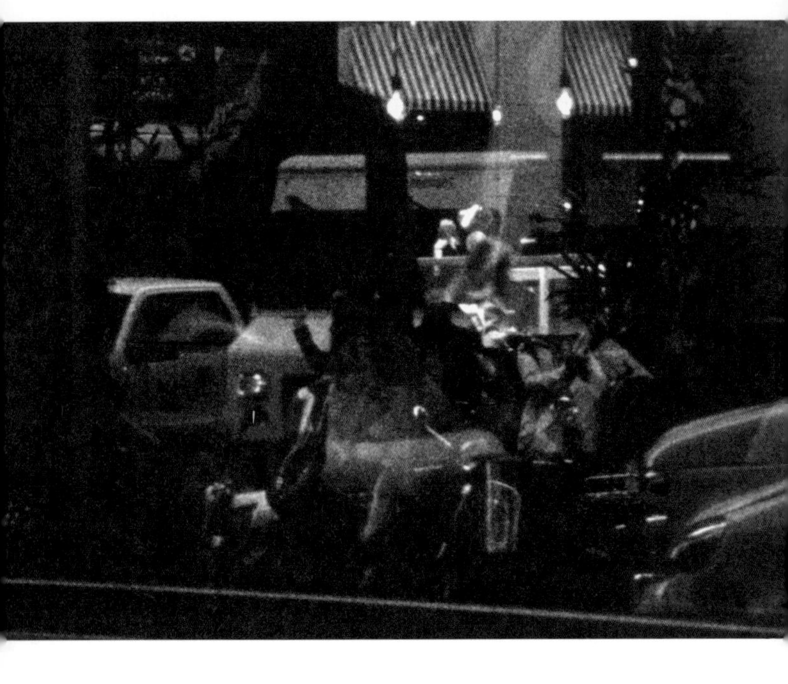

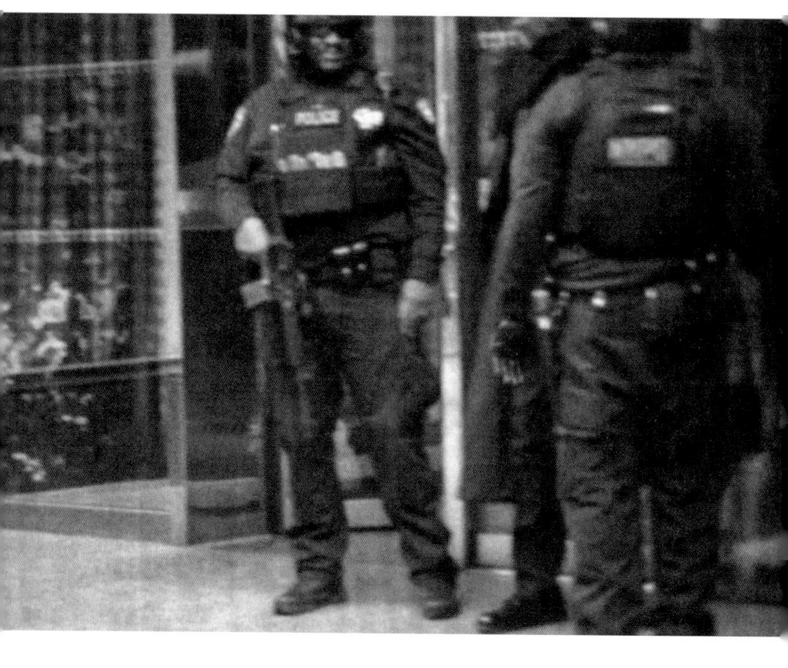

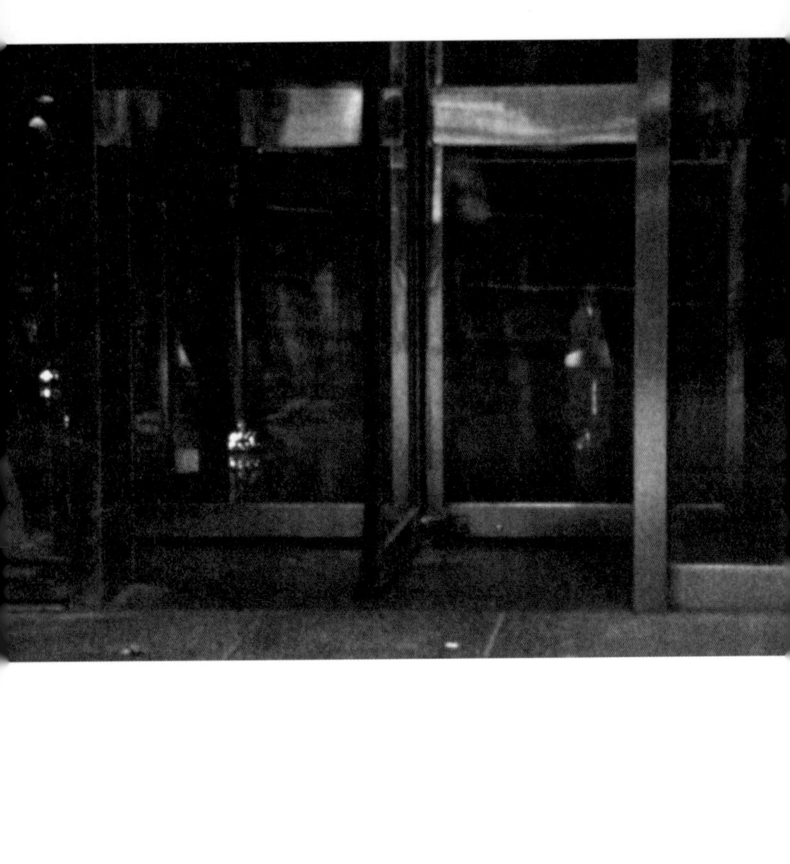

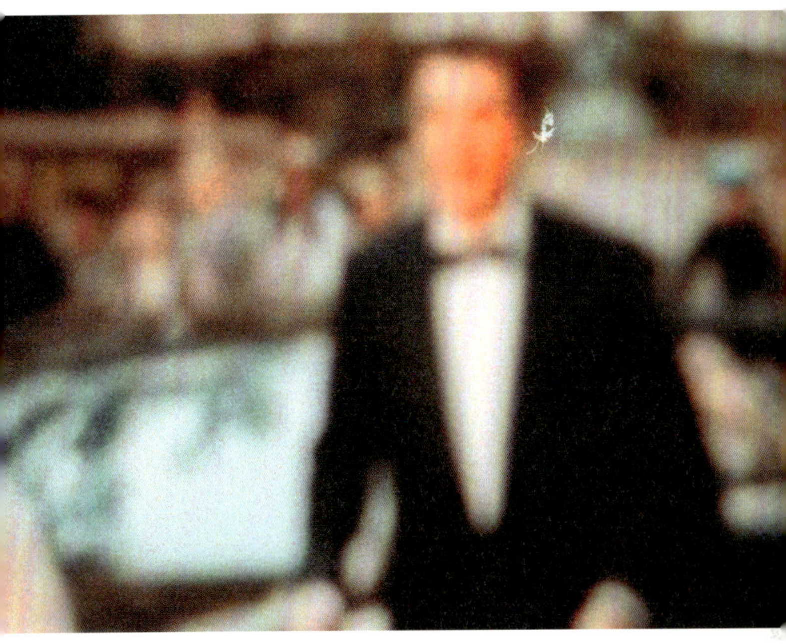

A long way from the *Litfaßsäulen*, the nineteenth-century columns constructed with at least a partial view toward public utility, cities continue to be remade in the image of advertisement. An understanding of the city gained by walking would inevitably encounter the increasing presence of advertising video screens. In subway stations, on either side of the train car doors, on the kiosk walls of the street vendor, bus stops, on what were formerly phone booths, taxi cabs, and even restaurant menus, everywhere the uncanny looped imagery in constant view of the pedestrian, seeking only to mimic their distracted attention span. Screens proliferate, and their size ever increases. In a renovation project undertaken after 9/11 a hall was constructed that houses a media property measuring well over four hundred square meters. It can be found beneath the Oculus, a structure designed by the architect Santiago Calatrava that houses the World Trade Center PATH train and connects Fulton Transit Center to Brookfield Place (Brookfield Place, formerly known as the World Financial Center complex, is constructed on top of a landfill

and is near the Battery Park City offices
of Goldman Sachs, Merrill Lynch, BNY
Mellon, and other financial institutions).
The stockbroker arrives from New Jersey
accompanied by these LED billboards
displaying distracting advertisements of
Lay's flipping in an unreal vacuum space, or,
alternatively, a group of trompe l'oeil
dancers performing in front of the white
marble walls of the shopping mall tunnel,
the projection seamless within the archi-
tectural structure. That certain types of these
screens also systematically surveil and
collect data regarding those who interact
with and pass by them make them fitting
targets during protest movements, where
they are regularly defaced.

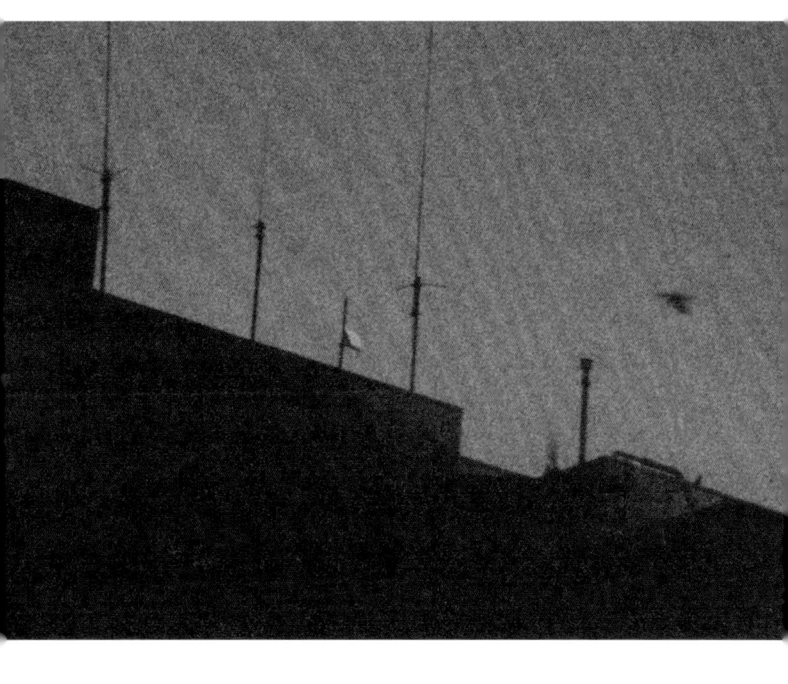

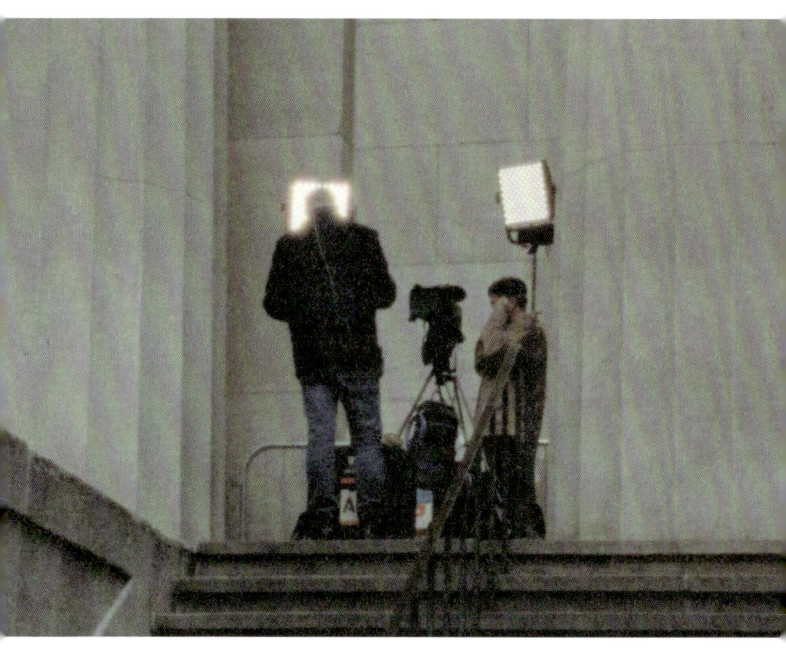

The form of the advertisement is
employed in *Professional witnesses.* and in
the construction of emblems inside light-
boxes, regularly shown alongside Bliss's
narrative works. In them what is on display
is not a product but images of the city in
disarray set alongside symbols of the corpo-
ration, shopfront, and worker. How else
for the conspirator to respond to a prepon-
derance of advertisements but to construct
emblems in opposition to the quickening
of every flow of information distractedly
consumed. In *Apple, Omelet* (2023) the brick
façade and boarded-up windows of an
Apple store on Prince Street are seen next
to a lamppost with traffic symbols over-
layed with a yellow that suggests for a brief
moment a distorted taxicab before a realization sets in that it is in fact the disjunctive
stock image of food preparation of the
type regularly seen at the twenty-four-hour
corner store. An ad blurs the imagination
of the city for its consumer, an emblem
responds. There is also Starbucks with a
double helix and a mannequin functionary
alongside the Western Union logo, seeming
to suggest the historical fact of the CIA's

surveillance of citizens who sent money through this service in the post-Patriot Act United States. Just as in the study of emblems, the re-purposing of signs in proximity to one another becomes a practice where symbols are recast and layered in order for them to speak a distinct language from the self-evident one they present.

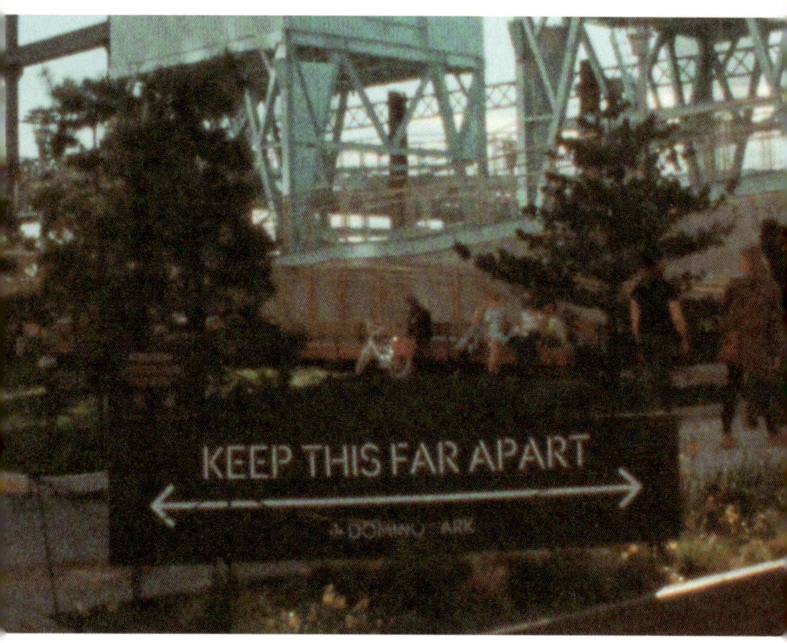

KEEP THIS FAR APART
A DOMINO PARK

I first encountered the work of Jenna Bliss in her May 2022 New York exhibition *HOMING*. At the time I was not aware of the many films, videos, and photographs that constitute her practice, and I was immediately taken by the presentation of the hour-long *Professional witnesses*. alongside the photographic works, *no artificial flavors* (2022). They seemed to coalesce with memories that were, at that time, for one reason or another, at the forefront of my mind. The video work in particular related so directly to an image from my childhood that when I had an opportunity to discuss it with the artist in her studio near the Financial District, I did not hesitate to go on and on regarding this connection in such a hurried manner that I'm not sure what impression I effected. I told her that the work had the exact presentation of a fever dream that had stuck with me since childhood, of an all-white void-like space where objects were suspended in a weightless environment, and that it was not only the visuals, but perhaps more importantly the texture of the spoken voice and the quiet that accompanied the testimonials and dialogue that had left a deep impression on me. Based on the Errol Morris *Switch* campaign for Apple, with its non-stop wood-block percussion soundtrack in order to sell the idea of the computer, Bliss's version foregoes a soundtrack outside of a brief nod alongside the title card and the silence becomes an attendant material that not only outlines the seriousness of the subject at hand, but also defamiliarizes the testimonials so as to rid the narrative of any overriding associations.

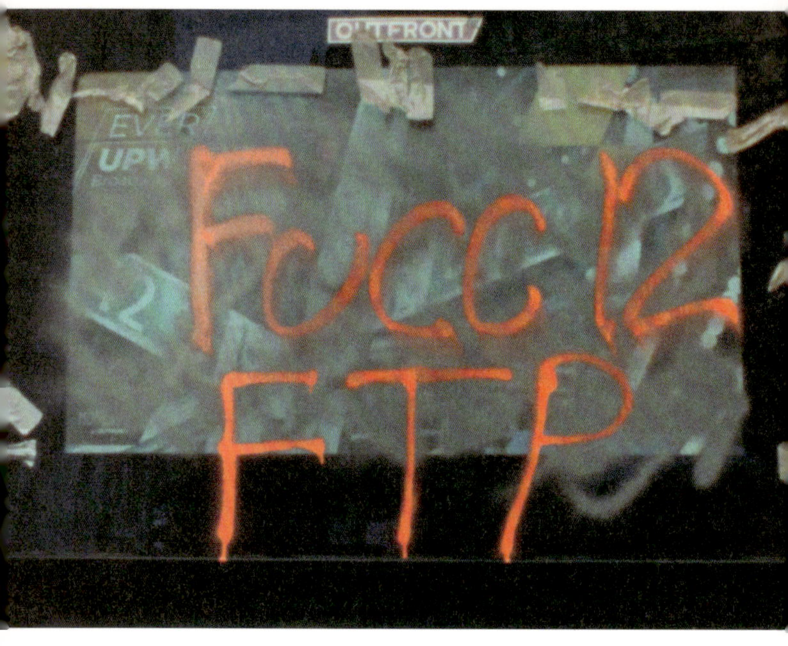
OUTFRONT
EVER
UPW
Fucc 12
FTP

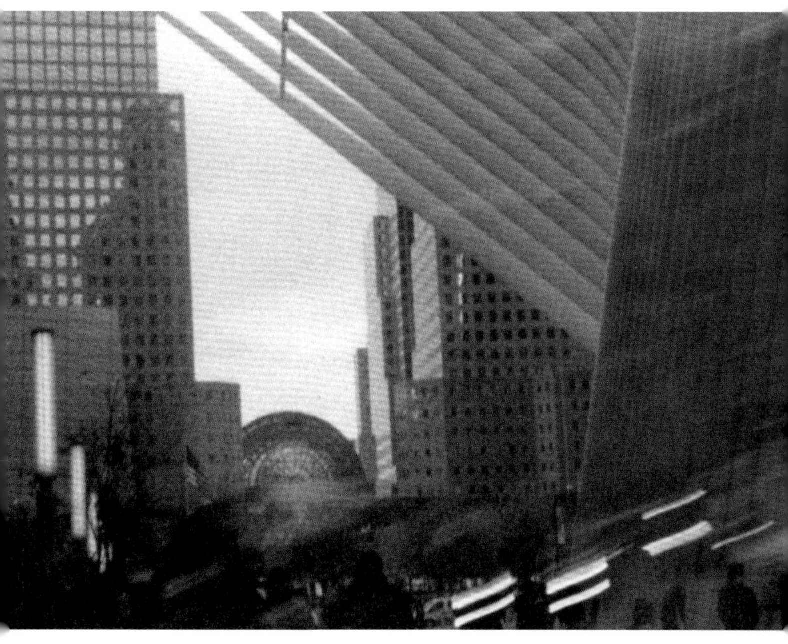

My enthusiasm for the work led to con-
versations with anyone who would listen,
and when I later mentioned this silence
to Susan Howe, she told me that in the late
1970s, when she was hosting a radio program from the Upper East Side where she
interviewed poets and critics, the experience
of physically editing the audio tape—splicing
and joining the material that was often
recycled from previous erased recordings—
led her to the discovery of a particular
phenomenon within the material itself. She
found that the tape would often retain
a physical trace of what had been erased
or dubbed over, that a ghost-like presence
could often be heard while delicately editing
in the audio booth. This presence would
not be evident to the listener of the final
broadcast, as the standardized volume for
radio would ensure that the "silence" was
left unheard, while the physical remainder,
for the person editing, would dictate the
composition of the program. Whereas the
silence in the final radio broadcast was
unintelligible, the remainder that I associated
with it became resonant across everything
I experienced thereafter as the exterior to

both the text and image Bliss's works presented, the historical residue of associations
made material within the films. This residue,
for both the artist as well as the audience,
recasts the reception of the information
conveyed within; it is the trace of the exter-
nal imagination of what is being described
that informs the construction of the work
and that allows for all the associations
of 9/11, the Wall Street crash, or indeed any
presented image of New York City at all,
to be read without overdetermination.

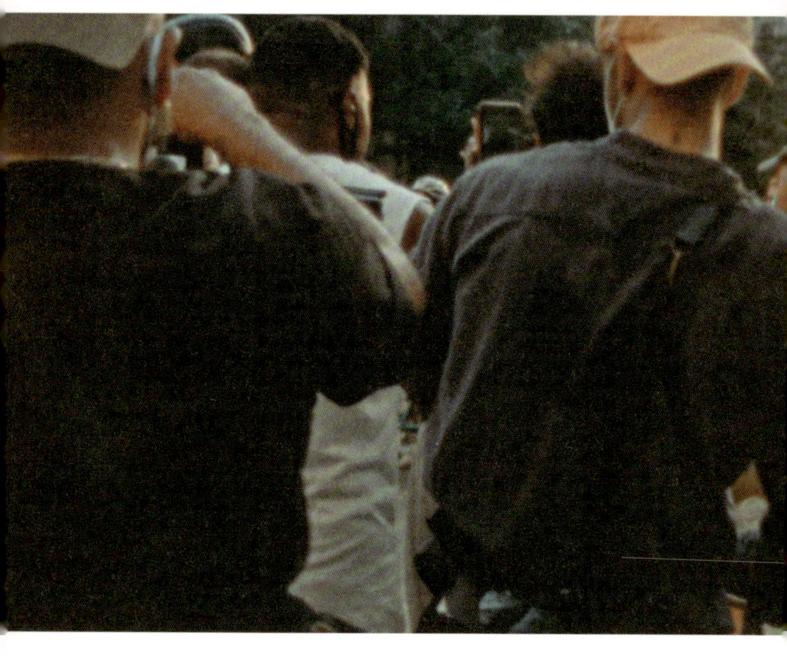

In one of her latest films Jenna Bliss confronts this remainder, residue, or fantasy, by couching the film in the proximate signifiers of the still dominant form of reality TV. *True Entertainment* is written in the style of a claustrophobic one-act play in anticipation of the financial crisis, though it could be casually broadcast between episodes of *Laguna Beach* or *The Hills*. It perfectly mimics the style of the period, its clichéd soundtrack, the clinking glass and swipe sound effects, the scripted "authentic" dialogue, the jumping camera, and the standardized thirty-minute length. Even the title speaks to a piece of entertainment as only another passing distraction in a completely market-driven world of exchangeable personalities, phrases, and occupations. Viewers of the work are confronted with the off-putting use of still-too-proximate recent fashions, slang, and now expired theoretical concepts. The audience laughs at the idea of art as a money laundering device but might also look around to wonder if it is okay to do so. *True Entertainment,* itself at risk of such a fate, dwells in this antagonism and casually sets insider trading and the shielding of assets squarely within the art market. The consequences of magazine-cut collages functioning as a tool for wealthy individuals to avoid taxes and launder illegal money (perhaps from weapons trading or insider bets) is finally met with the audience's awareness of what will likely soon occur to the young artist and gallery in the film. Hearing the representative name of the administration that forgave the crimes of the financial institutions is sufficient for the viewer to recognize the collapse that will soon occur: "Did you watch the debate with that Obama guy?"

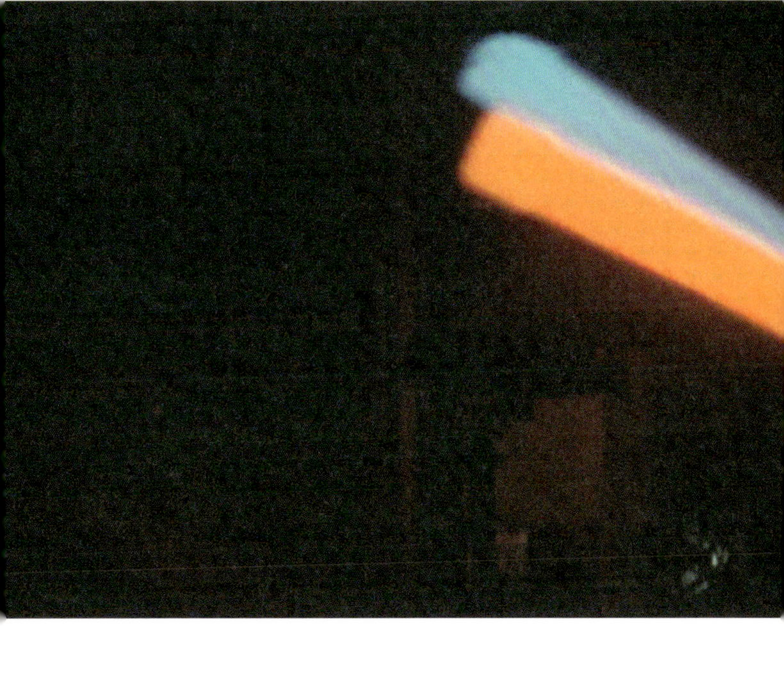

Bliss's works are cast in a manner that seeks historical legibility in a present reading, the same legibility that was sought by Benjamin in *The Arcades Project*, where images made from symbols, fragments, illustrations, and endless citations, would be capable of communicating unproblematically such things as the meaning of cities for its citizens, the reflection of water and sunlight in a building's panes of glass, or a bird's flight path navigating built structures where all that would remain is silence. One lightbox presents both a bird in flight, captured for a brief moment in fog just above the horizon, and a vessel capable of transporting the viewer past the intersection of Cedar and Broadway, over the construction grounds of the Calatrava, and finally landing on top of the Empire State Building.

Ivan Gaytan is a writer living in New York City.

Korrespondenz
Ivan Gaytan

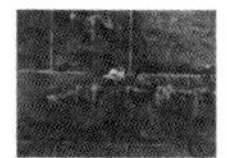

„In Zeiten des Terrors, wo jedermann etwas vom Konspirateur an sich hat, wird auch jedermann in die Lage kommen, den Detektiv zu spielen. Die Flanerie gibt ihm darauf die beste Anwartschaft.“[1]

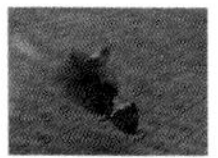

Von meinem Fenster aus sehe ich 200 West Street, 388 Greenwich, 60 Hudson Street, 33 Thomas Street und 32 Avenue of the Americas, letzteres ein Telekommunikationsgebäude, das einst die Western Union, AT&T und die New York Telephone Company beherbergte und heute in der Lobby einen Starbucks unterhält. In regelmäßigen Abständen werfen das One World Trade Center, das abends meist im Nebel verborgen liegt, und das Hotel Barclay 27 von links Schatten auf meinen Schreibtisch. Die Wahrnehmung von New York ist oft geprägt von einer Abfolge medial vermittelter Bilder, einer Fantasie, in der die Stadt den oben erwähnten Adressen ähnelt und einen spezifischen Moment in der Geschichte Lower Manhattans markiert. Sie wird darüber hinaus bestimmt durch Phänomene wie *Sex and the City*, die London-Platane (eine der tausend Arten, die zwischen 1939 und 1940 nach Robert Moses' Plänen für das Messegelände Flushing Meadows–Corona Park gepflanzt wurden), grünen Bänken und gelben Taxis, Woody Allen oder *The Real Housewives*. So werden das Sammeln und Zusammenstellen dieser Bilder, um ein Porträt der Stadt zu zeichnen, zu einem Werk der Montage.

1: Walter Benjamin, „Das Paris des Second Empire bei Baudelaire“, in: ders., *Gesammelte Schriften I*, hg. v. Rolf Tiedemann und Hermann Schweppenhäuser (Frankfurt am Main: Suhrkamp, 1991), S. 542 f.

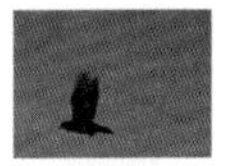
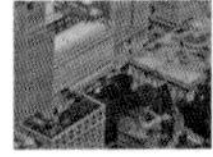
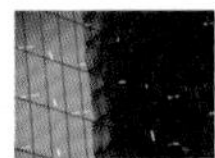

Ein Bild der Stadt findet sich auch in einer Reihe von Briefen aus den Jahren 1937 bis 1940: In einer Nachricht aus Dänemark vom 4. Oktober 1938 schreibt Detlef Holz an die Adornos, im Zimmer des Sohnes von Brecht hänge eine Karte Manhattans, die er gelegentlich aufmerksam studiere und anhand derer er sich ausmale, wie er die parallel zum Hudson River verlaufende Stra-ße ihrer Wohnung auf und ab gehe. Vielleicht stellt er sich auch die langsamen Bewegungen der Eisschollen vor, die man in jenem Winter vom Fenster im dreizehnten Stock der Exilwohnung von Gretel und Theodor Adorno aus sehen konnte, einer Wohnung voller Möbel aus Frankfurt und Berlin, darunter ein Schreibtisch mit Blick auf den Fluss, ein Glasschränkchen, ein Schreibma-schinentisch und ein Stuhl sowie eine Sammlung von Detlefs veröffentlichten und unveröffentlichten Aufsätzen, die bereits in den Vereinigten Staaten angekommen waren. Gretel Adorno, die Walter Benjamin seit ihren ersten Briefen aus dem Jahr 1933 mit seinem Pseudonym ansprach, schreibt ihm 1939, sie werde am Pier 88 auf seine Ankunft mit der SS Champlain warten und mit ihm das barbarische fremde Land und die Weltausstellung erkunden. Benjamin notiert mit Farbstift Routen und Adres-sen: 45 Christopher Street, 290 Riverside Drive, 429 W 117th Street. Er schreibt „Newyork" für New York City.

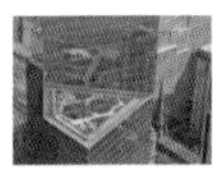
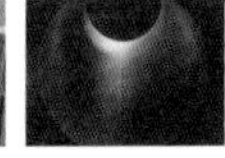

Die Korrespondenz über Benjamins mögliche Auswanderung und Übersiedlung in die Stadt und deren Scheitern fällt zusam-men mit der Sammlung einer Reihe von Notizen unter dem Titel

„Zentralpark", der Materialsammlung für *Das Passagen-Werk*
und den zahlreichen Überarbeitungen des Aufsatzes, der schließlich 1939 unter dem Titel „Über einige Motive bei Baudelaire"
in der *Zeitschrift für Sozialforschung* veröffentlicht wurde. Die
Ansätze aus dem Spätwerk Benjamins hätten gewiss in einer
Vorlesung über Ästhetische Theorie, die auf Einladung Meyer
Schapiros 1940 an der Columbia University hätte stattfinden
sollen, weiteren Ausdruck gefunden, und obwohl Benjamin diese
Vorlesung nie halten konnte, frage ich mich oft, was aus den
Ideen geworden wäre, wäre er in den 1940er Jahren wie vor-
gesehen durch die Stadt flaniert. Wie hätten sich die Bilder New
Yorks, wie sie in den Briefen zu finden sind, vereinbaren lassen
mit den fehlenden Eisschollen, „imposanten Turmhäusern",
dem Nebel, der die obersten Stockwerke zuweilen vollständig
umhüllt, den Taubenansammlungen unter Markisen und an
Straßenecken, dem waagerechten Mond oder der Abwesenheit
sämtlicher Sterne?

Im Sommer 1940 wurde sich Benjamin der Untragbarkeit
seines Planes, nach New York zu emigrieren, bewusst. Er woll-
te sich nicht trennen von der Bibliothèque Nationale und dem
Angelus Novus in seinem Wohnzimmer in der Rue Dombasle 10.
Er entschied sich weder für Jerusalem noch für New York, und
so blieb Paris trotz der sich verschlechternden politischen Bedingungen die einzige Alternative, um seine Arbeit an den *Passagen*
fortzusetzen. Der Lesesaal und die Druckschriftensammlung der
New York Public Library hätten es zwar nicht aufnehmen können mit einem Raum, in dem in greifbarer Nähe die Manuskripte
Victor Hugos aufbewahrt wurden, aber sie hätten vielleicht eine
Zeit lang genügt. Mit Gretel Adorno an seiner Seite hätte er
zweifellos unzählige Male die großen Dioramen der New Yorker
Skyline auf der Weltausstellung 1939/40 in Queens und die Werbe-
tafeln am Times Square besucht.

„Die Weltausstellungen verklären den Tauschwert der Waren.
Sie schaffen einen Rahmen, in dem ihr Gebrauchswert zurücktritt.
Sie eröffnen eine Phantasmagorie, in die der Mensch eintritt, um

sich zerstreuen zu lassen. Die Vergnügungsindustrie erleichtert ihm das, indem sie ihn auf die Höhe der Ware hebt. Er überläßt sich ihren Manipulationen, indem er seine Entfremdung von sich und den andern genießt."[2]

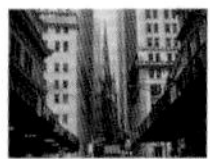

Benjamin verstand die Stadt Paris vermittels der Darbietung dessen, was in ihren Passagen zu finden war. Dort erschienen Objekte wie auf einer Bühne, erklangen allegorisch inmitten der in gläsernen Gängen um sie versammelten Mengen; sein Schreiben war geprägt vom Prinzip der Montage, die ihre präziseste Umsetzung in der ersten Fassung des Essays über Baudelaire fand. Und obwohl ich mir keiner besonderen Affinität der Künstlerin Jenna Bliss für das Werk Benjamins bewusst bin, lassen sich viele der Ansätze aus seinem Spätwerk in ihrer Darstellung der Stadt und deren jüngster Geschichte wiedererkennen: Benjamins Figur des Konspirateurs zeigt sich in Bliss' Auseinandersetzung mit Information und deren Austausch, seine Phantasmagorie dient

2: Walter Benjamin, „Paris, die Hauptstadt des XIX. Jahrhunderts", in: ders., *Gesammelte Schriften V*, hg. v. Rolf Tiedemann (Frankfurt am Main: Suhrkamp, 1991), S. 50 f. Dieser Paragraf erschien ursprünglich auf Französisch und in erweiterter Fassung: „Les expositions universelles idéalisent la valeur d'echange des marchandises. Elles créent un cadre où leur valeur d'usage passe au second plan. Les expositions universelles furent une école où les foules écartées de force de la consommation se pénètrent de la valeur d'échange des marchandises jusqu'au point de s'identifier avec elle: ‚il est défendu de toucher aux objets exposés.' Elles donnent ainsi accès à une fantasmagorie où l'homme pénètre pour se laisser distraire. A l'intérieur des divertissements, auxquels l'individu s'abandonne dans le cadre de l'industrie de plaisance, il reste constamment un élément composant d'une masse compacte. [...]" In: ders., *Gesammelte Schriften V*, „Paris, Capitale du XIXieme siècle. Exposé", S. 65.

als Antwort auf und wirkt in Verwendung von verschiedenen medialen Formaten und die Allegorie taucht auf in Form von Bliss' Verwendung des Fragments. In ihrem Werk wird ein Porträt der Stadt New York gezeichnet, das besonders zur Melancholie tendiert, geleitet von jenem Prinzip der Montage, das Benjamin in seinen Ausführungen über die Eisen- und Glaspassagen anwandte.

Bliss schreibt mit den Bildern, die sie bei ihren regelmäßigen Spaziergängen durch die Stadt aufnimmt. Durch den Einsatz der Montage, die sich als Strategie durch ihr gesamtes Œuvre zieht, inszeniert sie das Fragment als Teil einer umfassenden Erzählung. Jedes Bild wird zum Prolog eines im Entstehen begriffenen Werkes – als wäre das Fragment der Beweis einer größeren Handlung. In *Drone II* und *Drone III* (jeweils 2021) ist ein Teil des World Trade Center U-Bahnhofs zu sehen, der später in einer 8-mm-Aufnahme den Hintergrund eines fliegenden Vogels bildet. Dieser wiederum wird vom Bild eines Düsentriebwerks überlagert, bevor er schließlich auf einem Tisch eines nahegelegenen öffentlichen Platzes landet. Alles ist enthalten: das Bild eines Ortes und dessen Geschichte werden ebenso lesbar wie die wiederkehrende Flugbahn der Taube; die Zusammenhänge ergeben sich von Bild zu Bild und von Fotografie zu Fotografie. Die Bild- und Sprachfragmente in Bliss' Werk zeichnen eine Karte Manhattans, auf der ein Gebäude zum Symbol, zum Zeichen und schließlich zur Allegorie werden kann. Fakten tauchen ebenso schnell auf, wie sie aufgehoben werden. Bliss zeigt Oberflächen, die einerseits andeuten, was unter ihnen geschieht, welche Verschwörungen im Innern geplant werden, und andererseits Intransparenz und die vollständige Verschleierung von Informationen repräsentieren. In *Spectacle* (2021) arbeitet sie mit der Überlagerung von Bildmaterial, um eine allegorische Lesbarkeit der Skyline beziehungsweise der leer stehenden, spärlich beleuchteten Bürogebäude zu evozieren, und zeigt Schauplätze, die auch in *Professional witnesses.* (2021) auftauchen. Außerdem sehen wir Bilder der banalen Kommerzbauten rund um die Calatrava-Struktur des World Trade Center Transportation Hub, Bilder der New York Stock Exchange, des Monds, des Hudson River im Abendrot und die

105

Aufnahme eines von Hochhäusern gezeichneten Horizonts, der von einer Baustelle am Wasser aus gefilmt ist, die finanziert wurde von einem ehemaligen, mittlerweile aufgrund einer Kontroverse zurückgetretenen New Yorker Gouverneur. Auf dem eingezäunten Gelände raschelt Laub, kurz darauf setzt eine Taube zum Flug an. Bliss' Assemblage aus Firmenlogos, Geschäftsfassaden, Baugerüsten, Hausecken und Arbeiter*innen evoziert ein Bild der Stadt als Zentrum eines Imperiums im 21. Jahrhundert. Als Konspirateurin wirft sie Pläne, Verschwörungen, Entwicklungen und politische Figuren zusammen. Im ersten Abschnitt von „Das Paris des Second Empire bei Baudelaire" mit dem Titel „I. Bohème", schreibt Benjamin, der Konspirateur des 19. Jahrhunderts stelle die Barrikaden ins Zentrum seiner Bewegung: Es entstand eine Kommune, Kameraderie. Im 21. Jahrhundert rückt die Konspirateurin nun die Information selbst in den Mittelpunkt und ist in der Lage, die jüngste Vergangenheit New Yorks durch einige wenige Schlüsselbegriffe zu beschreiben: der 11. September, die CIA, Starbucks, Fluggesellschaftsaktien, Krongard. Die Referenzen sind tief in der präsentierten Konstellation verankert und fordern dazu auf – so die Anweisung des Videos *Connecting the Dots* – eins und eins zusammenzuzählen.

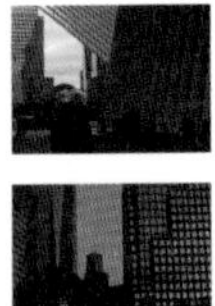

Bliss' Arbeiten streben eine Korrespondenz mit der gelebten Realität ihrer Aufnahmen an, im Bewusstsein der Künstlichkeit der Fotografie und der Dominanz des Spektakulären über das Visuelle – vor diesem Hintergrund ist auch ihre Entscheidung zu verstehen, die Formate von Reality-TV und Werbung zu replizieren. Ihr Werk wirkt der Abgelenktheit einer typischen Wahrnehmung von Werbung und Fernsehen entgegen. Stattdessen wird

deren anspruchslose Rezeption mit dem Diskurs der Konspirateurin konterkariert. Anstatt ein Produkt zu verkaufen, bedienen
sich die Arbeiten einer subtilen Sprache, die von Finanztrans-
aktionen, Waffenhandel und der Wall Street erzählt – wie in
der Zeugenaussage in *Professional witnesses*. („todo está junto,
con el gobierno, mucho noticiero, muchos periodistas …")
oder dem Hin und Her zwischen Sammlerin und Galeristen auf
einer Kunstmesse in *True Entertainment* (2023): „… full laundry service." Es handelt sich nicht um *Loose Change*, um Ver-
schwörungsfilme, sondern um gegenwärtige Bilder der Stadt in
der einfachen Sprache von Schauspieler*innen auf Bravo oder
MTV – oder aus Werbespots dieser Sender. Hier zeigt sich der
antagonistische Charakter der Werke: Es stützt sich auf das Wa-
renbild, destabilisiert es jedoch durch Verweise auf historische
Ereignisse in den Dialogen und die Forderung – wie sie sich
auch in den späteren Schriften Benjamins findet –, diese Bilder
nicht als Relikte einer toten Geschichte, als Propaganda oder
als bloße Fakten zu interpretieren, sondern sie durch ein „Jetzt
der Erkennbarkeit" zu betrachten. So schreibt Benjamin: „der
historische Index der Bilder sagt nämlich nicht nur, daß sie einer
bestimmten Zeit angehören, er sagt vor allem, daß sie erst in
einer bestimmten Zeit zur Lesbarkeit kommen. […] Nicht so
ist es, daß das Vergangene sein Licht auf das Gegenwärtige oder
das Gegenwärtige sein Licht auf das Vergangene wirft, sondern
Bild ist dasjenige, worin das Gewesene mit dem Jetzt blitzhaft zu
einer Konstellation zusammentritt. Mit anderen Worten: Bild ist
die Dialektik im Stillstand. […] Nur dialektische Bilder sind echt
geschichtliche, d.h. nicht archaische Bilder. Das gelesene Bild,
will sagen, das Bild im Jetzt der Erkennbarkeit trägt im höchsten
Grade den Stempel des kritischen gefährlichen Moments, wel-
cher allem Lesen zugrunde liegt."[3]

3: Walter Benjamin, „Das Passagen-Werk, Aufzeichnungen und Materialien:
N [Erkenntnistheoretisches, Theorie des Fortschritts]", in: ders., *Gesammelte Schriften V*, S. 577 f.

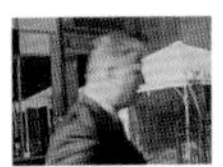

In der Träumerei des Flaneurs, in Bliss' Archiv der politischen Realität, des sozialen Lebens und der Lohnarbeit, wird ein Bild der Stadt ebenso unverstellt vermittelt wie auf einer Werbetafel am Times Square. Würde man wiederholt eine altbekannte Route durch die Stadt nehmen, wäre es nicht ungewöhnlich, den gesamten Prozess des Abrisses, der Brache und des anschließenden Neubaus eines Gebäudes mitzuverfolgen. Man könnte die Strukturen dahinter nachvollziehen, wenn man wüsste, welche Bauherr*innen das Bauvorhaben vorgeschlagen, welche Investor*innen es finanziert und welche Politiker*innen es genehmigt haben. Schließlich könnte man verfolgen, wie das Gebäude genutzt wird. Ist es Finanzhandel, ein neues Gefängnis, ein luxuriöser Wolkenkratzer, oder ein Einkaufszentrum? Die Entstehung der umliegenden Plätze wird vielfach durch Gesetze begünstigt, die es Immobilienfirmen erlauben, weiter in die Höhe zu bauen. Die gleichen Gesetze gestatten es Demonstrierenden, sich dort zu versammeln, zu organisieren und sie zu besetzen. Häufig wird anhand der Plätze und Parks der Kunstgeschmack der Immobilienfirmen im Hintergrund erkennbar: So findet man etwa Isa Genzkens *Rose III* und Mark di Suveros *Joie de Vivre* im Zuccotti Park oder Isamu Noguchis *Red Cube* auf der gegenüberliegenden Straßenseite. Die Oberflächen der Stadt bieten sich überall an, gelesen und entziffert zu werden. Bliss' Filmaufnahmen dokumentieren die vergangenen fünf Jahre und fangen die abstrakten Bedingungen gelebter Erfahrung ein, wie sie sich in protestgeschützten Eingängen, Co-Working-Spaces, an verspiegelten Glasfassaden und an von der *donor class* gestifteten Plätzen manifestieren. Die stillen Bilder suggerieren, dass wir eine exakte Fantasie der Stadt erzeugen können, fast so als würden wir uns in einen Kreisverkehr ein- und ausfädeln und uns in den konstanten Strom von Passant*innen integrieren, im Bewusstsein des stillen Einverständnisses, das den Verkehr auf den Gehsteigen und Straßen aufrechterhält.

„Die gegenständliche Umwelt des Menschen nimmt immer rücksichtsloser den Ausdruck der Ware an. Gleichzeitig geht die Reklame daran, den Warencharakter der Dinge zu überblenden. Der trügerischen Verklärung der Warenwelt widersetzt sich ihre Entstellung ins Allegorische."[4]

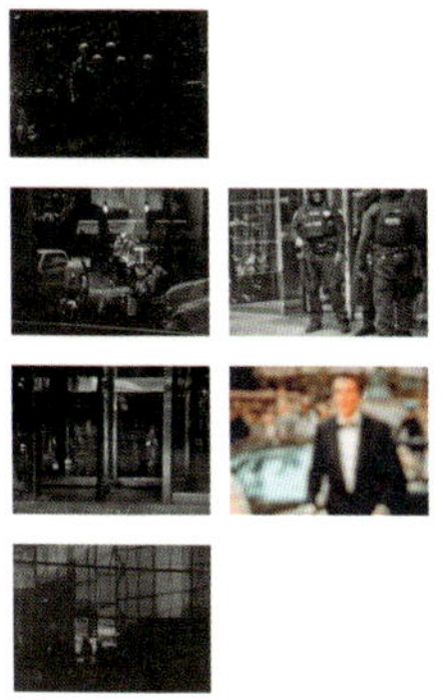

Auch wenn die Litfaßsäule, die im 19. Jahrhundert zumindest teilweise zum Nutzen der Öffentlichkeit eingeführt wurde, heute überholt scheint, ist doch bemerkenswert, dass Städte nach wie vor umgestaltet werden, um einem Bild der Werbung zu entsprechen. Wer zu Fuß durch die Stadt geht, stößt unweigerlich auf die zunehmende Präsenz von Werbebildschirmen. In U-Bahn-Stationen, auf beiden Seiten der Waggontüren, an Kioskwänden, Bushaltestellen, an ehemaligen Telefonzellen, in Taxen und sogar auf Speisekarten sind die unheimlichen Endlosschleifen im ständigen Blickfeld der Fußgänger*innen und passen sich deren abgelenkter, zerstreuter Aufmerksamkeit an. Bildschirme werden immer zahlreicher und immer größer. Im Zuge eines Renovierungsprojekts nach den Anschlägen des 11. September wurde für eine Medieneinrichtung eine über vierhundert Quadratmeter

4: Walter Benjamin, „Zentralpark", in: *Gesammelte Schriften I*, S. 671.

große Halle gebaut. Sie befindet sich unter dem sogenannten Oculus, einem Bauwerk des Architekten Santiago Calatrava, das die World Trade Center PATH Station beherbergt und das Fulton Transit Center mit Brookfield Place verbindet (Brookfield Place, ehemals bekannt als World Financial Center, wurde auf einer Mülldeponie errichtet und liegt unweit der Büros von Goldman Sachs, Merrill Lynch, BNY Mellon und anderen Finanzinstituten in Battery Park City.) Börsenmakler*innen, die aus New Jersey eintreffen, werden von LED-Werbetafeln empfangen, auf denen in einer Werbung für Lay's in einem Vakuum umherfliegende Kartoffelchips gezeigt werden. Manchmal sind es auch Tänzer*innen, die ähnlich einem Trompe-l'Œil-Effekt vor den weißen Marmorwänden der Mall auftreten, wobei die Projektion nahtlos in die architektonische Struktur übergeht. Einige dieser Bildschirme sammeln gleichzeitig systematisch Daten über diejenigen, die an ihnen vorbeigehen oder sie betrachten, und sind daher für Protestbewegungen ein beliebtes Ziel für Sachbeschädigung.

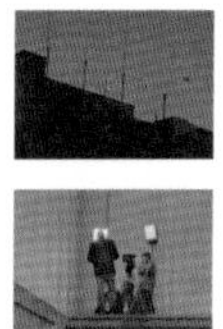

Bliss bedient sich nicht nur in ihrem Werk *Professional witnesses.* der Werbung, sondern auch in ihrer Serie von in Leuchtkästen ausgestellten Emblemen, die sie regelmäßig zusammen mit ihren narrativen Arbeiten zeigt. In diesen Leuchtkästen sehen wir anstelle eines Produkts die Stadt als Wirrsal, eine Kombination aus Firmenlogos, Schaufenstern und Arbeiter*innen. Wie auch sonst soll die Konspirateurin auf den beschleunigten Werbeüberfluss antworten, wenn nicht mit der Konstruktion von Emblemen, die sich dem Überfluss widersetzen? In *Apple, Omelet* (2023) sehen wir die Backsteinfassade und die mit Brettern vernagelten Fenster eines Apple-Stores in der Prince Street neben einer Straßenlaterne mit Verkehrszeichen, die von einem Gelb überlagert werden, das für einen Moment an ein verzerrtes Taxi denken lässt, bevor man erkennt, dass es sich um eine Stockfotografie eines Fertiggerichts handelt, wie man sie aus 24-Stunden-Shops kennt. Eine Werbung verzerrt die Vorstellung der Stadt für ihre Konsument*innen, ein Emblem antwortet. Dann sind da noch die Doppelhelix von Starbucks und eine kleine Figur neben dem Logo von Western Union, die auf die historische Tatsache zu verweisen scheint, dass die CIA nach der Verabschiedung des Patriot Act in den Vereinigten Staaten Bürger*innen überwachte, die diesen Dienst nutzten, um Geld zu verschicken. Die Umdeutung von Zeichen und die Analyse von Emblemen wird zu einer Praxis, in der Symbole in neue Kontexte gestellt und überlagert werden, sodass sie ihre ursprüngliche Sprache hinter sich lassen und beginnen, eine andere zu sprechen.

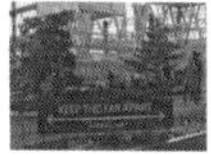

Das erste Mal begegnete ich Jenna Bliss' Arbeiten in ihrer Ausstellung *HOMING* im Mai 2022 in New York. Damals kannte ich ihre zahlreichen Filme, Videos und Fotografien noch nicht, war aber sofort eingenommen von ihrem einstündigen Film *Professional witnesses.* und den fotografischen Arbeiten *no artificial flavors* (2022). Sie schienen mit Erinnerungen zu verschmelzen, die damals in meinen Gedanken sehr präsent waren. Insbesondere die Videoarbeit hatte einen unmittelbaren Bezug zu einem Bild aus meiner Kindheit, sodass ich, als ich die Gelegenheit hatte, mit der Künstlerin in ihrem Atelier in der Nähe des Financial Districts darüber zu sprechen, nicht zögerte, ihr von dieser Verbindung zu erzählen. Ich bin mir nicht sicher, welchen Eindruck ich bei ihr hinterließ. Ich erzählte ihr, dass das Werk formal einem Fiebertraum meiner Kindheit glich: ein weißer leerer Raum, in dem Objekte in einer schwerelosen Umgebung

111

schweben. Aber es waren nicht nur die Bilder, die mich an meinen Traum erinnerten, sondern auch die Textur der Stimmen in den Dialogen, die mich faszinierten. Eine Referenz der Arbeit ist Errol Morris' *Switch*-Kampagne für Apple, in der ununterbrochen ein Holzschlagzeug-Soundtrack erklingt, um die Idee des Computers zu verkaufen. Doch in ihrer Version verzichtet Bliss, abgesehen von einem kurzen Einschub im Vorspann, auf Musik. Die Stille begleitet die Arbeit und unterstreicht nicht nur die Ernsthaftigkeit des Themas, sondern unterwandert auch die Zeug*innenaussagen und befreit die Erzählung von jeglichen übergeordneten Assoziationen.

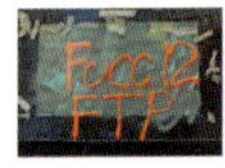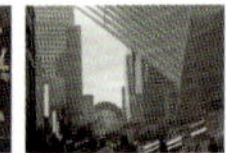

Meine Begeisterung für die Arbeiten führte zu Gesprächen mit allen, die bereit waren, mir zuzuhören. Als ich diese Stille in einer Konversation mit Susan Howe erwähnte, erzählte sie mir von einem Phänomen, das sie in den 1970er Jahren bei der Bearbeitung von Tonbändern entdeckt hatte. Für ihre Radiosendung, in der sie Interviews mit Dichter*innen und Kritiker*innen in der Upper East Side führte, benutzte sie oft Material mit alten oder bereits gelöschten Aufnahmen. Beim Schneiden der Bänder bemerkte sie eine geisterhafte Präsenz dessen, was gelöscht oder überspielt worden war. In der fertigen Sendung würden Hörer*innen diese Präsenz nicht wahrnehmen, da die Lautstärke des Radios dafür sorgt, dass die „Stille" ungehört bleibt. Doch die Rückstände haben einen Einfluss auf die Person, die das Material bei der Montage des Programms bearbeitet. Während die Stille in der fertigen Radiosendung also nicht mehr wahrnehmbar ist, hallte der Rest, den ich damit assoziierte, in allem nach, was ich danach erfuhr, in allen Texten und Bildern, die mir in Bliss' Werk begegneten: Der historische Rückstand der Assoziationen wird in den Filmen zum Material. Diese Rückstände verändern die Rezeption der vermittelten Information sowohl für die Künstlerin als auch für das Publikum. Es sind die Spuren einer Projektion von außen auf diese Information, die die Konstruktion des Werks prägen und Assoziationen mit dem 11. September, dem Börsencrash, ja mit allen Bildern New Yorks ermöglichen – allerdings ohne eine überdeterminierte Lesart.

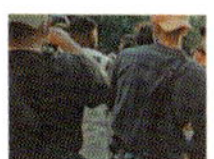

In einem ihrer jüngsten Filme konfrontiert Jenna Bliss Verbliebenes, Rückstände, beziehungsweise Fantasien, indem sie die Arbeit in die Nähe der noch immer verbreiteten Form des Reality-TV rückt. *True Entertainment* ist im Stil eines klaustrophobischen Einakters in Erwartung der Finanzkrise geschrieben, könnte allerdings auch beiläufig zwischen Folgen von *Laguna Beach* oder *The Hills* ausgestrahlt werden. Perfekt imitiert das Werk den Stil der Zeit, den klischeehaften Soundtrack, das Gläserklirren oder die *Swipe*-Soundeffekte, die vermeintlich authentisch geskripteten Dialoge, die ruckelnde Kamera, die standardisierte Länge von dreißig Minuten. Schon der Titel weist darauf hin, dass es sich um Unterhaltung handelt, die nur eine weitere vorübergehende Ablenkung in einer marktgesteuerten Welt austauschbarer Persönlichkeiten, Phrasen und Berufe darstellt. Betrachter*innen werden mit der befremdlichen Verwendung von gerade nicht mehr aktuellen Modetrends, Slang und überholten theoretischen Konzepten konfrontiert. Kunst als Mittel zur Geldwäsche – als Betrachter*in lacht man über diese Vorstellung und fragt sich zugleich, ob das unpassend ist. *True Entertainment*, selbst von diesem Schicksal bedroht, verweilt bewusst in diesem Antagonismus und stellt Insiderhandel und Vermögensschutz ganz beiläufig in den Kontext des Kunstmarktes. Betrachter*innen wird bald bewusst, was es für die Künstlerin und den Galeristen im Film bedeuten wird, dass wohlhabende Personen Collagen aus Zeitungsausschnitten als Mittel zur Steuervermeidung und zum Waschen illegaler Gelder (womöglich aus Waffenhandel oder Insiderdeals) genutzt haben. Die Betrachter*innen erahnen den nahenden Kollaps vielleicht schon im repräsentativen Namen der kommenden Regierung, die alle Verbrechen der Finanzinstitute vergeben werden würde: „Hast du die Debatte mit diesem Obama gesehen?"

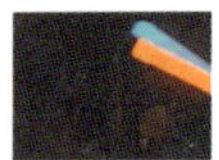

Bliss entwirft ihre Werke derart, dass ihre historische Lesbarkeit im Jetzt erkennbar wird, dieselbe Lesbarkeit, die Benjamin in seinem *Passagen-Werk* anstrebte und nach der Bilder, zusammengesetzt aus Symbolen, Fragmenten, Illustrationen und endlosen Zitaten, imstande wären, mühelos zu vermitteln, was Städte für ihre Bewohner*innen bedeuten, wie Wasser und Sonnenlicht in den Glasscheiben eines Gebäudes reflektiert werden oder wie ein Vogel durch gebaute Strukturen navigiert, in denen nur noch Stille herrscht. Einer der Leuchtkästen stellt sowohl den Flug eines Vogels, für einen kurzen Moment im Nebel gleich über dem Horizont eingefangen, als auch ein Transportmittel dar, das uns über die Kreuzung von Cedar und Broadway und über die Baustelle der Calatrava-Konstruktion führt und schließlich auf dem Empire State Building landen lässt.

Ivan Gaytan ist Autor und lebt in New York City.

All images: 2017–present, Super 8mm film, digital scans / Alle Abbildungen: 2017–
heute, Super-8-Film, digitale Scans

Works in the Exhibition / Arbeiten in der Ausstellung

Apple, Omelet, 2023
Found light box, Super 8mm film, pigment print / Gefundener Leuchtkasten, Super-
8-Film, Pigmentdruck   51.2 × 48.3 × 9.5 cm   Courtesy the artist and Felix Gaudlitz,
Vienna / Courtesy die Künstlerin und Felix Gaudlitz, Wien

Archive, 2024
Metal, fabric, Super 8mm film, dirt / Metall, Stoff, Super-8-Film, Dreck   Courtesy
the artist, Felix Gaudlitz, Vienna, and Ulrik, New York / Courtesy die Künstlerin,
Felix Gaudlitz, Wien und Ulrik, New York

Celine, Chocolate Pears, 2023
Found light box, Super 8mm film, pigment print / Gefundener Leuchtkasten, Super-
8-Film, Pigmentdruck   51.2 × 48.3 × 9.5 cm   Courtesy the artist and Felix Gaudlitz,
Vienna / Courtesy die Künstlerin und Felix Gaudlitz, Wien

Chanel, Orange, 2023
Found light box, Super 8mm film, pigment print / Gefundener Leuchtkasten, Super-
8-Film, Pigmentdruck   51.2 × 48.3 × 9.5 cm   Courtesy the artist and Felix Gaudlitz,
Vienna / Courtesy die Künstlerin und Felix Gaudlitz, Wien

Documents, 2024
Super 8mm film, digital c-print / Super-8-Film, digitaler C-Print   20 × 36 cm
Courtesy the artist, Felix Gaudlitz, Vienna, and Ulrik, New York / Courtesy die
Künstlerin, Felix Gaudlitz, Wien und Ulrik, New York

Drone I, Drone II, Drone III, 2021
Silver gelatin prints / Silbergelatineabzüge   Each / je 114.3 × 78.2 cm   Courtesy the
artist and Felix Gaudlitz, Vienna / Courtesy die Künstlerin und Felix Gaudlitz, Wien

Duane Reade, Tomato Sauce, 2023
Found light box, Super 8mm film, pigment print / Gefundener Leuchtkasten, Super-
8-Film, Pigmentdruck   51.2 × 48.3 × 9.5 cm   Courtesy the artist and Felix Gaudlitz,
Vienna / Courtesy die Künstlerin und Felix Gaudlitz, Wien

Eurodollars, 2024
HD Video TRT   4:29 min.   Written with / Geschrieben mit James Duesterberg
Courtesy of the artist, Felix Gaudlitz, Vienna, and Ulrik, New York / Courtesy die
Künstlerin, Felix Gaudlitz, Wien und Ulrik, New York

no artificial flavors #1, #3, #4, #5, #7, #10, #11, #12, #13, #14, #15, 2022 Silver
gelatin prints, painted metal frames / Silbergelatineabzüge, lackierte Metallrahmen
Each / je 20 × 25 cm   Courtesy the artist and Ulrik, New York / Courtesy die
Künstlerin und Ulrik, New York

Now vacant. (remix), 2021
HD Video TRT   3:29 min.   Courtesy the artist and Felix Gaudlitz, Vienna /
Courtesy die Künstlerin und Felix Gaudlitz, Wien

Panorama I, Panorama II, 2021
Silver gelatin prints / Silbergelatineabzüge   Each / je 55.4 × 152.4 cm   Courtesy
the artist and Felix Gaudlitz, Vienna / Courtesy die Künstlerin und Felix Gaudlitz,
Wien

Professional witnesses., 2021
SD/HD Video TRT   56:32 min.   Courtesy the artist, Felix Gaudlitz, Vienna,
and Ulrik, New York / Courtesy die Künstlerin, Felix Gaudlitz, Wien und Ulrik,
New York

True Entertainment, 2023/24
Video   29:30 min.   Courtesy the artist and Felix Gaudlitz, Vienna / Courtesy die
Künstlerin und Felix Gaudlitz, Wien

This book is published on the occasion of the parallel exhibitions *Jenna Bliss*, curated by Anna Gritz, and *Carol Rhodes*, curated by Beatrice Hilke, at Haus am Waldsee (February 2 to May 5, 2024). / Diese Publikation erscheint anlässlich der parallelen Ausstellungen *Jenna Bliss*, kuratiert von Anna Gritz, und *Carol Rhodes*, kuratiert von Beatrice Hilke, im Haus am Waldsee (2. Februar bis 5. Mai 2024).

The Haus am Waldsee thanks the artist, the author, the exhibition's contributors, and those individuals who wish to remain anonymous. The artist thanks Anna Gritz, Ivan Gaytan, Eva Wilson, James Duesterberg, Michèle Graf, and Selina Grüter. / Das Haus am Waldsee dankt der Künstlerin, dem Autor, den Mitwirkenden der Ausstellung sowie den Personen, die anonym bleiben möchten. Die Künstlerin dankt Anna Gritz, Ivan Gaytan, Eva Wilson, James Duesterberg, Michèle Graf und Selina Grüter.

Exhibition / Ausstellung

Haus am Waldsee e.V.
Director / Direktorin: Anna Gritz
Managing Director / Geschäftsführer: Tobias Bader
Curator / Kuratorin: Beatrice Hilke
Curatorial Assistant / Kuratorische Assistenz: Pia-Marie Remmers
Press and Communications / Presse und Kommunikation: Erik Günther
Digital Communications / Digitale Kommunikation: Sarah Mohr
Accounting / Buchhaltung: Wiebke Sünderhauf
Education / Vermittlung: Yvonne Zindel with / mit Linus Cuno von Aufsess,
Luise Bichler, Valentin Hesch, Mette Kleinsteuber, Martina Kutsch,
Johanna Pistorius, Claire Rüffer, Anna Schulte
Visitor and Event Manager / Besucher*innen- und Veranstaltungsmanagerin:
Regina Schreieder
Install / Aufbau: Sebastian Jefford, Carl-Oskar Jonsson, Frederik Worm
Gardener / Gärtnerin: Nele Schinz
Intern / Praktikantin: Sarah Albrecht
Front Desk and Invigilators / Kasse und Aufsicht: Michael Gottberg,
Samer Ismail, Jeannette Mügge, Swenja Schmidt

Publication / Publikation

Editor / Herausgeberin: Anna Gritz (Haus am Waldsee)
Managing Editor / Redaktionelle Leitung: Eva Wilson
Texts / Texte: Ivan Gaytan, Anna Gritz
Translation / Übersetzung: Michèle Graf, Selina Grüter
Copy-editing / Lektorat: Anna Siebold, Tina Wessel, Eva Wilson
Design / Gestaltung: Benedikt Reichenbach
Lithography / Lithografie: Max Color
Print / Druck: Medialis, Berlin

Published by / Publiziert von:
Haus am Waldsee, Argentinische Allee 30, 14163 Berlin
T +49 30 80 18 935, info@hausamwaldsee.de, www.hausamwaldsee.de
Spector Books, Leipzig, www.spectorbooks.com

First edition / Erste Auflage
ISBN 978-3-95905-840-7
Printed in Germany / Gedruckt in Deutschland

Distribution / Vertrieb:
Germany, Austria / Deutschland, Österreich:
GVA, Gemeinsame Verlagsauslieferung Göttingen GmbH&Co. KG,
www.gva-verlage.de
Switzerland / Schweiz: AVA Verlagsauslieferung AG, www.ava.ch
France, Belgium / Frankreich, Belgien: Interart Paris, www.interart.fr
Great Britain / Vereinigtes Königreich: Central Books Ltd,
www.centralbooks.com
North, Central, and South America, Africa /
USA, Kanada, Mittel- und Südamerika, Afrika:
ARTBOOK/D.A.P., www.artbook.com
South Korea / Südkorea: The Book Society,
www.thebooksociety.org
Japan: twelvebooks, www.twelve-books.com
Australia, New Zealand / Australien, Neuseeland:
Perimeter Distribution, www.perimeterdistribution.com

Haus am Waldsee is led by /
Das Haus am Waldsee wird getragen durch:
Haus am Waldsee e.V.
Board / Vorstand: Jakob Braeuer, Kaspar v. Erffa, Leonie v. Gadow

The project is generously funded by /
Das Projekt wird großzügig gefördert durch:

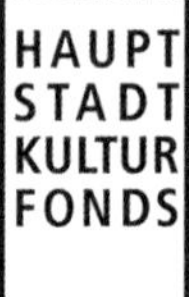

Haus am Waldsee
Freunde und Förderer

Haus am Waldsee is generously funded by /
Das Haus am Waldsee wird großzügig gefördert durch:

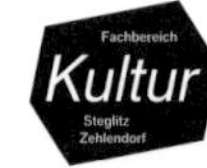